T0093498

metadata
matters

John Horodyski

CRC Press
Taylor & Francis Group
Boca Raton London New York

CRC Press is an imprint of the
Taylor & Francis Group, an **informa** business

AN AUERBACH BOOK

Some material has been inspired by the author's own blog and work, facilitated workshops and seminars, his teaching, and his regular contributions to CMSWire, which provides daily updates on digital customer experience, digital workplace technologies and practices, and intelligent information management.

First Edition published 2022
by CRC Press
6000 Broken Sound Parkway NW, Suite 300, Boca Raton, FL 33487-2742

and by CRC Press
2 Park Square, Milton Park, Abingdon, Oxon, OX14 4RN

© 2022 John Horodyski

CRC Press is an imprint of Taylor & Francis Group, LLC

ISBN: 978-1-032-03924-4 (hbk)
ISBN: 978-1-032-03923-7 (pbk)
ISBN: 978-1-003-18973-2 (ebk)

DOI: 10.1201/9781003189732

metadata matters

If data is the language upon which our modern society will be built, then metadata will be its grammar, the construction of its meaning, the building for its content, and the ability to understand what data can be for us all. We are just starting to bring change into the management of the data that connects our experiences.

Metadata Matters explains how metadata is the foundation of digital strategy. If digital assets are to be discovered, they want to be found. The path to good metadata design begins with the realization that digital assets need to be identified, organized, and made available for discovery. This book explains how metadata will help ensure that an organization is building the right system for the right users at the right time. Metadata matters and is the best chance for a return on investment on digital assets and is also a line of defense against lost opportunities. It matters to the digital experience of users. It helps organizations ensure that users can iden-tify, discover, and experience their brands in the ways organizations intend. It is a necessary defense, which this book shows how to build.

About the Author

John Horodyski is a Managing Director with Salt Flats, with executive management strategy experience in infor-mation management, including digital asset management (DAM), metadata and taxonomy design, content strategy, analytics, governance, MarTech, and marketing operations. John is one of the world's leading experts on metadata and DAM and has provided strategic direction and consulting for a variety of Fortune 10, 50, 100, and 500 clients from Consumer Packaging Goods and Retail to Media & Enter-tainment, the Pharmaceutical industry, and Insurance.

Advance Reviews

"Digital technology has become our externalized nervous system. Our mental activities are closely linked to the quality and organization of the data we produce and consult on a daily basis. For our work to be effective and well-coordinated, it is necessary that our metadata system be fit for purpose and regularly updated. John Horodyski's book *Metadata Matters* is an impassioned plea for intelligent metadata management. It is a must read for Chief Information Officers, Chief Data Officers and anyone concerned with sound knowledge management."

— *Pierre Lévy*, PhD, Fellow of the Royal Society of Canada, CEO of INTLEKT Metadata Inc.

"Metadata guru John manages to pull off the difficult task of writing a book that's not only much needed and useful but also highly engaging. In lucid prose, using rich examples from our personal and professional lives, John makes a strong case for metadata and its central role for your digital strategy. You'll learn how metadata can increase the return on investment of marketing and content systems. There's practical guidance, best practices and more to put all this knowledge into practice as well. A must read for marketing, content, and digital professionals."

— *Kashyap Kompella*, CEO, RPA2AI Research

"Metadata is about making information accessible, and John Horodyski has made the subject of metadata accessible to all in this very readable book that not only teaches principles of metadata but also increases our awareness and appreciation of metadata. Drawing on his rich experience as consultant, Horodyski thoroughly addresses metadata in all fields and industries. This book is not limited to those who plan to manage their metadata but is for anyone who wonders whether they need to or whether they should even care."

— *Heather Hedden*, Author, *The Accidental Taxonomist*

"From helping us make our everyday choices to making our machines smart, metadata powers our world. John's book is a love song sung to the stuff that's about stuff, full of stories that will entertain you and examples that will help you understand, craft, and choose metadata that indeed matters."

— *Louis Rosenfeld*, co-author of *Information Architecture* and publisher and founder, Rosenfeld Media

"In what is certain to be a seminal work on metadata, John Horodyski masterfully affirms the value of metadata while providing practical examples of its role in our personal and professional lives. He does more than tell us that metadata matters—he vividly illustrates why it matters. As a Digital Asset Management (DAM) and Metadata Expert, Horodyski is uniquely aware that metadata itself is an asset that is needed to provide context so that other information can be located, retrieved, managed, and interpreted. He distinguishes among different types of metadata—descriptive, administrative, and structural—and discusses the usefulness of metadata standards to provide consistency which can facilitate findability, migration, and interoperability, as well as result in cost savings. Whether new to the concept of metadata or veteran metadata specialists, by the end of the book, all readers will be metadata champions!"

— *Patricia C. Franks*, PhD, CA, CRM, IGP, CIGO, FAI
President, NAGARA
Professor Emerita
San José State University
San José, CA, USA

"Finally, an easy-to-read handbook that explores how metadata can inspire us to unlock the potential of the information we create. In *Metadata Matters*, John Horodyski delivers practical, real-world examples of how putting metadata to work can help us develop differentiating capabilities that would be otherwise difficult or impossible to enjoy. Do yourself a favor. Get this book and devour every chapter. You'll discover how effectively using metadata can dramatically advance the role of content across your enterprise."

— *Scott Abel*, The Content Wrangler

Note from the Author:

It's so meta.

Really, it is. Meta is what it is all about. Meta this, and meta that. The currency and relevancy of meta are ever present and participatory in our cultural and technological discourse, with recent announcements on the "race to the metaverse"—the unknown, much hypothesized next version of the internet, with virtual and augmented reality experiences, with Facebook®, Microsoft®, and gamers charting courses for this arguable meta unknown.

The very word "meta" itself has a fascinating epistemology from its origin as a prefix defining the "aboutness" of something. It is often noted as a "prefix"— that is, a word put before another word, to denote being "after" or "beyond." And it is this evolution of the term in a more modern usage to define something above and beyond in pop culture: to describe when something is being self-aware. It is more than the thing itself, exhibiting as a higher level of perspective of aboutness.

If the "meta" amplifies the experience, then before we go falling forwards into any meta experience, and, in particular, the metaverse, we should figure out how to manage the real one in which we all currently live and operate. Technology be damned; we are still fumbling around our real-world scenarios with real-world issues such as privacy, information disorder, and echo chamber–based algorithms. The metaverse will be just that—a meta-amplification of what we are currently doing and the extension of even more, with virtual worlds as inspired by digital gaming to help influence future, unwritten digital experiences. Is it the next chapter of social connection? Or, is it yet another place of social confusion, distraction, or angst with no compass or markers, either intellectual or technological, to guide our actions. Meta-good? Meta-bad? Meta-other?

As a nod to chaos theory and the perils of science without responsibility and ethics, remember the ominous warning from fictional character Dr. Ian Malcolm in the 1993 film Jurassic Park, *"Your scientists were so preoccupied with whether or not they could, they didn't stop to think if they should."* Just because you can, doesn't mean you should, but yet here we are on the precipice of change to a world with a metaverse and uncharted and untested new digital experiences.

The concern is that this anticipated metaverse will replicate the worst of what we already experience on the internet. We are all raised on content from books to television to the internet to the aggressive proliferation of social media and connections. Before we can even figure out the information disorder of our current use of the internet and social media technology, we have meta-problems that we are not "meta-solving" right now. In its current guise, the creation, dissemination, and consumption of information in 2021 has become hyper-personal, targeted, and influential.

If data is the language upon which our modern society will be built, then metadata will be its grammar, the construction of its meaning, the building for its content, and the ability to understand what data can be for us all. We are just starting to bring change into the management of the data that connects our experiences in recent General Data Protection Regulation (GDPR) legislation in Europe and state-sponsored privacy laws within the United States. This is the start of meta-goodness for our future.

I never met a data I didn't like, and I look forward to a future where data has been grounded in good governance and the ability to present itself as accurate, authoritative, and authentic. Metadata—data about data and yet so much more—is the foundation for your digital strategy. You want your content to be discovered, to be found and experienced in the way in which it was intended. Access is everything. Classification is meaningful. But what will a metaverse give us except exclusion and disorganization? More of the same that we have now but in an unknown realm in which to operate. If you have great content and no one can find it, the value of the content is nonexistent. The path to good metadata design begins with the realization that your digital assets need to be identified, organized, and made available for discovery, and metadata will help ensure that you are building the right system, for the right users, at the right time. Metadata done well will ensure that you and your content will never be lost again.

Metadata matters because it defines us at any given point in time with the best information available to us by means of its managed foundation for content clarity. Metadata is the defense needed against our current information disorder, and the pathway through which our individual and collective "aboutness" and "awareness" may serve us all well. It's that good because it's so meta.

Dedication

To Ben and Kate.

Contents

List of Figures and Tables

Acknowledgments

Thank you.

I wrote this book to communicate and inspire others about metadata.

I started writing this book in Palm Springs in January 2020, with many starts and stops along the way, with some significant pandemic writing time, and it was eventually completed with these acknowledgments in November 2021. The in-between and unbelievable pandemic times included many late-night writing sessions fueled by determination and will, and the music of Tame Impala, to morning writings powered by espresso and Brian Eno. Writing this book was a labor of love.

Amidst the good busyness of it all, with work and teaching and life, I devoted the time to write on weekends and evenings, sacrificing much to do so. During these writing periods, I was reminded that many things do indeed matter . . . your family and friends, your health and well-being, and the business of life.

Thank you Ben and Kate, for being there along the way with your love and laughter, especially when it mattered the most. Your creativity, courage, and determination bring me everlasting joy. Thank you Mom and Dad, who will always be my greatest champions forever.

Thank you to my friends Dr. Ken Haycock, Marian De Gier and John B. Webster, Tony Green, Perry Hewitt, Vida Morkunas, Cristina Aguilera, Belle Ancell, Craig Thomas, Ken Best, Rick McNabb, Deb Marksberry, and Ryan Murphy for your friendship, leadership, and continued support in all that I do.

Thank you Mark Pottie, for teaching me that a healthy body requires a healthy mind, and encouraging me not only to set goals, but to think stronger in order to be stronger.

Thank you to my Insights & Analytics team, who are an ongoing source of inspiration and encouragement with the great work they do in helping make the world be more organized, accessible, and meaningful.

Thank you to my Metadata and DAM colleagues, whose phone calls, texts, emails, and in-person meetings helped me along the way. Our meaningful metadata musings have proven invaluable over the years, and I look forward to many more in the future.

Finally, thank you to my DAM students at the School of Information at San José State University over the last 14 years, who continue to inspire me and my work.

Thank you to DoorDash and UberEats, who made the pandemic that much easier.

Thank you Vancouver, to the great baristas at Matchstick, the cookies at Delany's, the Vesper martinis from the Hawksworth Lounge, and the fresh oysters, vodka sodas, and beach view from the patio at Hook Sea Bar.

Thank you Whister-Blackcomb for the many alpine hikes, the invigorating cardio, and après-hike cocktails at the Mallard Lounge at the Fairmont Chateau Whister.

Thank you NYC, for the Americanos and occasional Cortados from the great baristas at La Colombe in NoHo, lunches at Via Carota with Siobhan, Friday drinks at the Stonewall, singing songs at 2:00 a.m. at Marie's Crisis, and pierogi at 3:00 a.m. at Veselka's.

Thank you LA, for the collaborative and collective intelligence procured at the Beverly Hilton poolside lounge, impromptu meetings at the Abbey, and weekend lounging and scootering in Abbot Kinney.

Thank you Palm Springs, for the never-ending supply of sunshine and positive poolside happiness at the Alcazar, for the morning coffees at Koffi, afternoon drinks at Chill Bar, singing songs at Quadz, and long, meaningful dinners at Workshop.

Thank you all for making this matter.

— John Horodyski
Palm Springs, California
November 2021

About the Author

John Horodyski, MLIS, MAS, is a digital sleuth, author, pundit, librarian, archivist, strategist, and management consultant who loves many grand things. These include a great cup of coffee, the splendor of long breakfasts, the grandeur of long dinners, the luscious libations of champagne, a Negroni in summer, a Manhattan in winter, and vodka sodas with lime anytime (but not necessarily in that order), the subtle sublime sounds of minimalist piano and chillout, the principled positive power of metadata, the never-ending necessary life skill and joy of reading books, the physical and spiritual benefits of hiking in the mountains, and the beauty that can only be found anywhere in the Mediterranean, the island of Naxos, the Spanish Riviera, the Sunshine Coast of British Columbia, the Big Island of Hawaii and Hapuna Beach, and the warm desert sun and midcentury extravagance of Palm Springs for good living for my future home.

John is a Managing Director with Salt Flats, with executive management strategy experience in information management, including digital asset management (DAM), metadata and taxonomy design, content strategy, analytics, governance, MarTech, and marketing operations. John is one of the world's leading experts on metadata and DAM and has provided strategic direction and consulting for a variety of Fortune 10, 50, 100, and 500 clients from Consumer Packaging Goods and Retail, to Media & Entertainment, the Pharmaceutical industry, and Insurance. John is also an Adjunct Faculty member at San José State University, where he teaches a graduate course in DAM. In addition to regular training and public speaking on digital media and metadata, John is a board member/metadata editor of the *Journal of Digital Media Management* and a monthly DAM contributor to CMS Wire.

John lives in Vancouver, Canada, for now.

Chapter 1

In Praise of Metadata: Lost and Found

1.1 An Airplane Saga

I fly on airplanes. A lot.

In fact, I fly more than a lot. I travel pretty much each week to one of my regular business destinations where my clients are situated. From New York City, to Los Angeles, Chicago, Washington DC, Vancouver, Toronto, London, Amsterdam, and on it goes. As a frequent flier, I am fortunate to receive premium levels of membership for airlines for which such status affords me premium seating and all things associated with "premium" for airlines. You can most often find me in 2A, the window seat of course, either working away on my laptop, reading a book, or gazing out the window for inspiration at 34,000 feet. This is forced luxury at its finest.

I consult with large corporations on their management of information; their digital assets; and, more importantly, the information about their assets—their metadata. Whatever it may be—television shows, consumer products, or marketing materials—I work with and consult on how to better organize their assets for improved identification, distribution, use, and reuse, both internally within their organization and externally to the public and to all those consuming and using their assets. As a librarian and an archivist, I have made my living helping others organize and be organized in their business systems and processes. I have been described as a metadata guru, a taxonomist, a librarian, and a digital sleuth . . . all true at various points in time, and all factual as regards my efforts to help organize information. Metadata is critical for findability and discovery, for if your assets are not organized in any meaningful way, they cannot be found. And, without question, they want to be found.

A unique event last year brought forth a new travel experience for me with another business trip which started out so well from my flight from Atlanta to New York City, and looking forward to touching down at La Guardia to then head home and settle in for a bit of respite. And, as usual, I was comfortably seated in 2A, this time on an airline (name protected to preserve the innocent) with four rows of first class, two-by-two, thereby equally 16 passengers at the front. Upon boarding the plane, I found my seat, tossed my laptop on it, and then placed my carry-on luggage in the overhead bin. My luggage is a standard black Tumi of carry-on luggage measurements, with a black Aeroplan Super Elite luggage tag, which has stood by me for many years. A few scrapes and scars, but it certainly has aged well. The flight was comfortable, no turbulence to speak of, and I was able to get some emails written thanks to the Wi-Fi on board. The plane landed on time, taxied to the gate, and parked for the night. Then the adventure began.

As the plane parked and the perfunctory and well-understood arrival bell rang, we all rose like members of a courtroom, ready for action. Most stretched, others yawned, but all raised their hands to the overhead bin to grab their carry-on luggage and go. So, that's what I did . . . but my luggage was not there. My initial response, and truly the only response I had at the moment, was, "That's impossible." There were only 12 of us here in first class, and it could not have gone astray during the flight. So where was it? I could sense the urgency of those folks in rows 3 to 6 who also wanted to get up and go, but I stood there staring at the bin, wondering what sort of incredible magic trick this could be. If it were only a rabbit in the hat, but it was my luggage . . . my clothes, my toiletries . . . my essentials for life on the road.

As the flight was not full, there were only four passengers ahead of me in the first row. Surely, they would not have taken my bag, as they already had their own . . . how odd that would be. And then I noticed a piece of luggage in my bin that was rather more charcoal than black and, in fact, quite smaller than mine. And upon a further look, it was quite roughed up . . . certainly not my luggage. But yet, there it sat, untouched, and in splendid isolation in the overhead bin, as everyone else pushed by me and made their way off the plane. Something was just not right, and that charcoal, scruffy-looking luggage was now part of my experience, whether I wanted it to be or not. The choice was not mine.

By this time, all of first class had exited the plane, and economy class was halfway through their exit ritual. The only thing I could do was speak to Kate, the service director at the door, who had been so great to me and all the other passengers during the flight. I walked up to her and proclaimed, "I think we have an interesting situation here." "Mr. Horodyski," she said, "whatever is the matter?" "Well," I exclaimed, "my luggage appears to be missing." "What?" she gasped. "That's impossible. Are you sure? How could that be?" Emphatically, I agreed, all the while beginning to worry that something strange, not necessarily evil, but strange was going on.

"Is there a chance that someone took my bag by accident?" I asked. "Oh my, no, that never happens," Kate responded. It was at that moment that we both looked at each other and realized that perhaps this was the first time for each of us when the normal rules of business travel might well have been broken. Our eyes locked in confusion and a slight twinge of despair, then slowly we turned our heads to the overhead bin.

She pointed to the bin and said, "Is that not your bag?" To which I exclaimed, "No, it certainly isn't." Of course, I had not actually checked that bag firsthand, but I was confident it was not my bag. So I reached up to take the bag down. Without a doubt, it was not my bag. Not only did it not look like my bag, but it was as light as a feather, probably only 10 pounds or so . . . hardly enough for more than three days of travel.

As I placed the luggage on the floor and raised the handle to steer it down the aisle, I noticed a tag. Not my black Aeroplan Elite tag, but a tag nonetheless, weathered and worn, and with the name Adam Smith (name changed to protect the guilty, or innocent, depending upon your point of view). I wheeled the luggage to Kate and proclaimed, "This is NOT my bag." This fact was now clear. There was no innuendo, no circumstance, and no confusion. All data elements were there to show that this was a fact.

"Oh no," gasped Kate, "how could this be? I can't believe it." "Well, believe it," I said, "this is not my bag, but Adam Smith's bag. I want my bag back. How do you suppose we might accomplish this request?" She threw her hands in the air and shouted, "Yes. Adam Smith! He was the elderly gentleman seated in 1B ahead of you. I remember him." At that moment, she moved into action and said, "Let's go! We can do this. We can find your luggage, as it must be with Adam Smith," Immediately, she grabbed the airplane phone and called the check-in desk.

So there we were—Kate, myself, and Adam Smith's charcoal, weathered, and worn luggage—exiting the plane and rushing to the check-in desk.

As I watched Cheryl, the attendant at the check-in, desk turn on the computer, it was if I heard Han Solo arrogantly boast, "Watch this!" as he ignited the Millennium Falcon into hyperdrive. I was both cautiously optimistic and eagerly curious to see where this digital sleuth work could lead. "Let's find Mr. Smith and what he is all about," Cheryl pronounced. And sure enough, by a few keystrokes on the computer, Cheryl retrieved the flight manifesto and was able to find Adam Smith's name. But that was just the beginning. She then clicked on his name and was able to see more information about Mr. Smith, including his address and phone numbers. "We have a home phone number and a cell number for him, so let's try the cell number, as he has to still be here in the airport." And that's exactly what she did—she called Mr. Smith on his mobile phone. "It's busy," she said and quickly added, "he must be here in the airport talking on the phone. So, let's try Plan B," Cheryl concluded. "Let's phone his home number to try and get a message to him." So, that's what she did. Cheryl now had access to such powerful data about Adam Smith that she was able to use this for our common good.

She dialed his home phone number. "Hello," answered a pleasant-sounding woman. "Is this Mr. Adam Smith's residence?" asked Cheryl. "Yes, it is," the caller responded, "I am his wife, how might I help you?" "It's Cheryl Jones from the airline, and we are trying to locate your husband. It appears that he has taken someone else's luggage by accident, and we need to get it back." "Oh dear," exclaimed Mrs. Adam Smith, "that's not good to hear; are you sure?" "Yes, ma'am, I am pretty confident that there has been a mistake made with the bag." It was at that moment that Cheryl used her camera phone to show the luggage to Mrs. Adam Smith. There was a slight pause, and then she responded, "Well, my goodness. Yes, you are correct. I am so sorry. That is not my husband's luggage . . . it looks like it, but yes, the tag is clearly not his . . . it is John Horodyski's. That's what the tag says." Accessing the metadata about Adam Smith and my bag had solved our dilemma.

1.2 Metadata Matters

Metadata matters because it gives structure and meaning to the data associated with all that we do in our business and personal transactions.

Metadata matters because it is both identification and discovery; it's about access.

Metadata matters because it tells you where your content came from, where it is going, and how it can be used.

Metadata matters because it is the foundation of your content. Metadata is more important than we know: it defines our personal and business data, and yet it is still mysterious and not as well known as it should be. Metadata development is a strategic imperative in the endeavor to effectively manage and exploit a company's content and knowledge. The successful implementation of any content-related strategy—for data, digital assets, or text—requires implementation of a holistic metadata schema that is supported by technology, people, and process. Metadata increases the return on investment of a content system by unlocking the potential to ingest, discover, share, and distribute assets.

This book is both an appreciation of metadata and a way in which to share the value and importance of metadata. The more we understand something, the better we are able to appreciate it and use it wisely in our personal and business affairs. Metadata, like language itself, is a reflection of all of us . . . it is both subjective and objective at the same time, as it tries to define who we are, what we are doing, when we are/were doing it, how, and why. It is not immune to race and gender bias, and to ageism and opinion, but with good governance metadata responds as society evolves and reflects a more respectful understanding of the human condition and the content it creates.

Metadata is specific. Metadata is general. Metadata describes all that we have so we may better understand what it is and what we need to do, providing as much meaning as possible. The opportunity for content owners, marketing technologists—all those managing content—is in understanding the value metadata provides to their assets and how it can empower their digital operations from creation, through discovery, to distribution. Metadata is the best way to protect yourself and defend your digital assets from information anxiety and mismanagement. If a good offense is your best defense with metadata as with anything else, then it is worth investing the time, energy, and resources to identify, define, and organize your assets for discovery. Metadata serves asset discovery by:

- Allowing assets to be found by relevant criteria
- Identifying assets
- Bringing similar assets together
- Distinguishing dissimilar assets
- Giving asset location information

Content is no longer "queen" . . . there are many in the realm, not the least of which is the user and the user experience. If you have great content and your users cannot find it, the value of the content is diminished or lost altogether. You need to understand how your users and customers want to interact with your assets before designing your metadata schemes. If you carry those user needs through to the back-end data structure, you'll empower users with the categories and content attributes they need to filter and find what they want. I had one piece of black carry-on luggage that was now with someone else, and I wanted that luggage returned to me.

Metadata, by definition, is simply data about data. But it is so much more than that. It is the descriptive, administrative, and structural data that defines an asset, whether that asset is a photograph, a video, or even our unique and personal identification attributes. Metadata comprises the elements that keep us together and provides a frame of reference for our own discovery. Sometimes, it is good to have those elements, the technical "bits and bobs," working for us, because sometimes that is all we have to work from, and when put together, through categories and associations, we are able to formulate an identification—a meaning. It is those very elements which define ourselves and our assets and provide meaning both in content and in context. No one, or no thing, wants to get lost.

1.3 Metadata in Three Acts

Metadata had its first public display of affection and curiosity in 2012, when then former CIA Director David Petraeus and his lover, Paula Broadwell, were found to have had an illicit affair after an FBI investigation investigating email records[1]—a dramatic revelation due to what may be seen as a rather undramatic record: metadata. The term itself was not necessarily new, but its use in media was, and its association with not just data but specifically personal data made it all the more interesting and alarming. The federal government's searches and requests for personal data was alarming then as it is now, but add in the fact that such global massive internet search engines and social platforms as Google® and Twitter® also monitor data on an ongoing basis.

What is known as a *Transparency Report*[2] was first created in 2010 by Google, then in 2012 by Twitter, then by others over time. The value in these

---

[1] Hodson, H. (2012, November 16). How metadata brought down CIA boss David Petraeus. NewScientist.com. https://www.newscientist.com/article/dn22511-how-meta data-brought-down-cia-boss-david-petraeus/

[2] "A transparency report is a statement issued on a regular basis by a company, disclosing a variety of statistics related to requests for user data, records, or content. Transparency reports generally disclose how frequently and under what authority governments have requested or demanded data or records over a certain period of time. This form of corporate transparency allows the public to discern what private information governments have gained access to through search warrants and court subpoenas, among other methods. Some transparency reports describe how often, as a result of government action or under copyright provisions, content was removed. Disclosing a transparency report also helps people to know about the appropriate scope and authority of content regulation for online discussions. [1] Google first launched a transparency report in 2010, with Twitter following in 2012. Additional companies began releasing transparency reports as during the aftermath of the global surveillance disclosures beginning in 2013, and the number of companies issuing them has increased rapidly ever since. Transparency reports are issued today by a variety of technology and communications companies, including Google®, Microsoft®, Verizon®, AT&T®, Twitter, Apple®, Dropbox®, Facebook®, Yahoo!®, and CloudFlare®. Several companies and advocacy groups have lobbied the U.S. government to allow the number of secret data requests (requests which include a gag orders—including National Security Letters) to be described within ranges in the report." Wikipedia. https://en.wikipedia.org/wiki/Transparency_report

reports shows, among many things, the increase that the US government makes in requests for data on users' accounts—observing data, arguably seen as surveillance with data. An argument later strengthened by Edward Snowden in his biography *Permanent Record* states that, "[M]etadata can tell your surveillant virtually everything they'd ever want or need to know about you, except what's actually going on inside your head."[3]

In a second example, the 2013 United States Senate Intelligence Committee, reporting on the programs and activities of the Intelligence Community, was a turning point in the history of metadata. The word itself, *metadata*, was now thrust upon both the media and the public discourse as an important word, although one often misunderstood, but important enough to warrant both curiosity and fascination as to what it is, what it does, who is doing it, and what can be done with it. In particular, the discussion of the National Security Agency's (NSA) collection of telephone records is a captivating read on many a good subject, including intelligence, surveillance, and data . . . subjects worthy of review then as now in 2021, as the increasingly powerful use of data has come under serious scrutiny by public and private bodies alike. The most interesting statement provided in a news conference from a senior senator on the committee was, "This is just metadata. There is no content involved," referring to the NSA's bulk collection of Americans call records.

"*There is no content involved.*"

This is a most profound statement—not necessarily egregious in nature, and not inflammatory, but ill conceived. At a rudimentary level, not only did the senator not fully understand the intricate nature of metadata realty, either at a singular or, more importantly, a collective level, but also simply was not aware of the power and meaning of metadata in our information society—our digital and physically recorded society.

Metadata has a place all to itself in the management of information and needs to be better understood by everyone who creates, disseminates, and uses data, content, information, and ultimately knowledge. I have never met the good senator, but if I had the opportunity, I would suggest we go out for a drink. Perhaps a nice aged, dignified, peaty, and balanced whiskey with the slightest of medicinal hints of warmth. Good adjectives, and great metadata, of course. And I would tactfully explain why that statement could not be more wrong, for in fact metadata is everything. It is the power that enables our content and makes content what it is and purports to be.

The third act of metadata occurred in 2013 with Edward Snowden and the United States NSA, when he copied and leaked classified and sensitive information from the NSA during his time as an employee of the United States Central

---

[3] Snowden, E. (2019). *Permanent Record*, p. 180. New York: Metropolitan Books.

Intelligence Agency (CIA). In a 2016 article authored by Paul Szoldra at *Business Insider*, the leaked document "highlights the collection of phone metadata as one of the agency's 'most useful tools.'"[4,5] Szoldra further explained how the document leaked by Snowden, and then published by The Intercept, "says that the NSA has used metadata such as numbers called, IP addresses, and call duration to yield 'concrete results.'"

The long-term effect of what Snowden did was to bring the discussion of metadata not just to the forefront of government, business, and the individual, but also to the realization that data is a powerful tool for use in many ways that affect the security and privacy of data and those in its association. In this instance, *IP addresses*—numeric labels assigned to each device connected to a computer network that uses the IP (internet protocol) for communication—was the unique metadata that identified an activity or event that could be monitored. Metadata can be many things to many people in what needs to be identified, understood, and then discovered, and the collection of so much data via communications technology has many opportunities for investigation.

Metadata matters because we interact with it each and every day in both our professional and personal lives. We need to know and understand more about it and care about what metadata is and the power it has to find what we are looking for in our content. We collect data to make meaning, and then we use that meaning in order to allow for some form of access, whether it be to track or record events, to analyze trends over time for decision-making actions, and to provide the information back to others seeking knowledge. Surveillance itself is a harsh word, with arguably negative connotations due to its suspect intentions, but the observation of data for whatever reason does occur. For instance, when you write a letter in MS Word, you are willingly (or unwillingly, depending upon your knowledge of the IT security in your organization) working with metadata. An easy click on File → Properties → Summary shows you the metadata fields that are associated with your work (see Figure 1.1).

Author's note: Do you ever wonder how your name got there anyway?

When I show this Properties table to clients and attendees in presentations and workshops, the overwhelming reaction is shock and awe not only in that it exists, but why they were not aware of it, when did it start (or how long has it been there), and worse for some, who put their name there and who is watching this.

---

[4]   Szoldra, P. (2016, December). Leaked NSA document says metadata collection is one of agency's "most useful tools." Business Insider. www.businessinsider.com/nsa-docu ment-metadata-2016-12

[5]   *State and Surveillance* by David Lyon offers a great overview of data surveillance and the use of metadata. https://www.cigionline.org/articles/state-and-surveillance

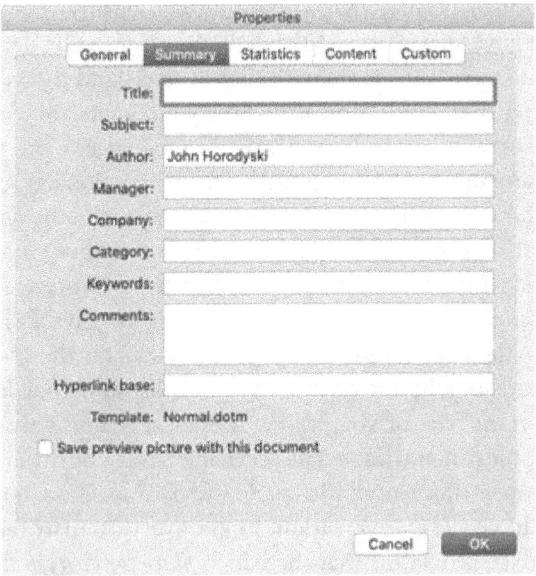

Figure 1.1   Typical Properties Table

We are being tracked, and our activities are being watched, as much as we are tracking ourselves and our own activities. We use metadata to help us organize our folders on our computers, so we have somewhere to place our files, so we may one day use them again in our work. We describe and organize our music into playlists that match our feelings and emotions so we may find them again. You, above all, know your assets and what they can do for you. Defining a strategy demands that you collaborate with those who best know the systems and other resources needed to release your assets' potential.

Content is varied and needed for many reasons, and as long as change exists in your business, your strategy will change—it is never really "finished." Metadata is a program, not a project. It has no finite end, as it is ongoing and needs to be managed as such with resources, financial considerations, and fair planning. And, as metadata is associated with language, then that too strengthens the argument that the work of metadata is never done. Language is not dead—nothing could be further from the truth. It is alive and well and prospering in our content-rich and cluttered society. This past year of 2020 proves this so well with great new additions to our lexicon, including:

- PPE
- Curbside pickup
- Super spreader

It is important to be prepared for this and to ensure that your solution is flexible and well governed. Successful collaboration starts by defining what your customers and business want to do with digital assets and then creating the plan to achieve it. After that, communicating how your assets are used to drive business will inspire others—from IT staff to all users present and future who seek to innovate those assets for future use. It's access in action.

Metadata increases the return on investment of a content system by unlocking the potential to ingest, discover, share, and distribute assets by applying systematic organization. Metadata is the best way to protect and defend digital assets from content clutter and mismanagement. Invest the time, energy, and resources to identify, define, and organize assets for discovery. Yes, sorting belongings by category better clarifies your needs, and that is why metadata is such an important part of your work. Metadata brings value to your assets, making them not just identifiable but accessible. You know that assets are critical to business operations, and you want them to be discovered at all points within a digital life cycle from creation, to discovery, to distribution.

A wise old adage proclaims that there is *"a place for everything and everything in its place"*[6]—in fact, this is one of the major tenets of library and information science and the practice of classification. Access is everything. Classification is meaningful. Action is needed now for the volume of digital assets on our desktops, storage drives, shared drives, collaborative spaces, and content repositories throughout the corporate structures created to manage content. Think about the digital experience for users and about ensuring that they can identify, discover, and experience *brand* the way in which it was intended. It is a necessary defense. Integrity of information means it can be trusted as authentic and current. If we define an asset as something that has value to the organization and is needed by others for use and reuse in their work, then it is clear that we should place positive controls on access to ensure it may be found and used.

Discovery does not always have to be an accident, and metadata provides the framework or support by which everything may be found in its right place. Something more is needed in order to make it all work; a word is sometimes not enough, and we need more—perhaps, a descriptive word or words in order to find that something we seek. What happens if content is only described as "miscellaneous," or "whatever" . . . could you find what you are looking for? You may well be able to find it, albeit through a confusing and challenging

---

[6] "This proverb is variously associated with Samuel Smiles, Mrs. Isabella Beeton, and Benjamin Franklin. *The Oxford Book of Quotations* dates it from the 17th century. Such a reference is usually accurate, although the authors supply no evidence for their assertion. If correct, it would pre-date all of the above notables." https://www.phrases.org.uk/meanings/14400.html

process, and it may well take a long time to do so, which leaves a negative user experience, and one you may not wish to repeat. Imagine walking into a public library with the predetermined and conscious intent of looking for *Jane Eyre,* by Charlotte Brontë, and instead finding all the fiction books, including "Victorian Literature" and "823.8"[7] books, in a pile on the floor. We need classification and structure in order to help our discovery process. You only get what you give, so give meaning to what you have. And that's what metadata does for us: it's the meaning and the ability to provide access not only by giving meaning to something, but by allowing that meaning to be found by someone else.

If we accept that language is alive, then we must accept that language will grow, evolve, and change over time. Some things need to change as a matter of respect, and other things change as a matter of sociopolitical cultural changes in the words we use and their meanings. Take, for example, the common phrase, "And, the winner is," familiar to many award shows and events; it begs the question of who or what is a winner after all. After 1988, the phrase was changed to, "And, the Oscar goes to," after show producer Allan Carr decided to make it less "competitive." The argument may be made that everyone is indeed a winner, as they are nominated for a particular category, but only one recipient may receive the actual Oscar. The new phrase is indeed more "accurate" in terms of cause and effect.

Similarly, during the AIDS epidemic in the 1990s, the term *VD*, which stood for venereal disease, became *STD*, which stands for sexually transmitted disease, to avoid the connotation of something "dirty."[8] Furthermore, it was then changed around 2013 to become *STI,* or sexually transmitted infection, to indicate a shift away from the stigma associated with the word *disease*. These examples show that words do indeed have meaning and change with societal norms.

A last example, the term *cisgender* was first seen in academia in the 1990s but did not gain momentum until 2007, when transgender theorist Julia Serano used it in her book *Whipping Girl*,[9] and it then caught on in the popular medium and was eventually added to the *Oxford English Dictionary* in 2015.[10]

---

7 https://www.librarything.com/mds/823.8—Melvil Decimal System: 823.8; Wording: Literature > English > Fiction > Victorian period 1837–1900.

8 https://english.stackexchange.com/questions/161621/when-did-venereal-disease -become-sti

9 Serano, J. (2007). *Whipping Girl: A Transsexual Woman on Sexism and the Scapegoating of Femininity*. Seal Press. 9781580051545.

10 McIntyre, J. (2018). What does it mean to be 'cisgender'? The Sydney Morning Herald. https://www.smh.com.au/lifestyle/life-and-relationships/what-does-it-mean-to-be-cisgender-20180920-p504y2.html

In a more contemporary setting, the social media hashtag # is just metadata in drag. Rising in popularity since 2007 on Twitter,[11] the hashtag is a form of user-generated content (UGC) tagging that enables identification and cross-referencing of content sharing for a subject or theme. It is a positive exaggeration of a descriptive attribute as a means to give respect, identity, and attention to one's presence on social media, applicable to a personality as much as to a brand. In fact, the effective use of good hashtags on social media has had a direct influence on product managers and brand managers alike, monitoring "image" and "use" by consumers, then feeding that information back inside the walls of the business to better understand how a brand is being discussed and used. This usage has the unique potential of transferring some of that key knowledge back into product design evolution as a means of better reflecting consumer behavior and demand for meaning . . . well, how very metadata.

Arguably, can one be too attached to a classification or category, such that it can be associated with the use of a word—for example, *label*—which in itself has a more negative connation than, say, the word *tag*? A label is a classifying phrase or name applied to a person or thing, especially one that may well be inaccurate or restrictive, whereas a tag may be seen as more neutral, as something used for identification or location.

Language is messy at times, because we are all figuring it out together in real time, and that's okay so as long as everyone agrees with the premise that language is alive and evolving and that we may strive to work together to bring an effective, respectful, and inclusive meaning to the words we use. The origins of our words may well come from academia or science as much as they do from popular culture with slang. We should always be looking to provide better access to our content. Be mindful of your audience, be responsive to their changing needs, and ensure you govern that change. Ultimately, we all want to find what we are looking for, whether that be our identity, our status, or our luggage.

Metadata matters. More needs to be known.

1.4 Metadata in Action

Some personal, professional, pertinent metadata elements: John Horodyski is a cisgender male, digital sleuth, managing director, management consultant, librarian and archivist, son, brother, father, global citizen and Canadian, who loves to do exemplary work with his clients, hot coffee, perpetual breakfasts with

---

[11] Lips, A. (2018, February 20). History of hashtags: How a symbol changed the way we search & share. Social Media Week. https://socialmediaweek.org/blog/2018/02/history -hashtags-symbol-changed-way-search-share

good people for good conversations, *Stolichnaya* vodka and sodas with a lime on the side in summer, a Manhattan with Rye (*Bulleit Rye* Frontier Whiskey) in the winter, a delicious Syrah from the Russian River valley all year long, a crisp Pino Gris from the Okanagan always, chillout music, metadata, reading a book a week, the warmth and love that Palm Springs provides, and the beauty of the 808 state of Hawaii.

Metadata Elements

Name	John Horodyski
Title	Managing Director
Year	2021
Organization	Salt Flats
Age	48
Primary Location	Vancouver, BC, Canada
Alternative Location	New York, New York
Preferred Location	Palm Springs, California
Secondary Location	Airplane
Most played song	"New Person, Same Old Mistakes"—Tame Impala—iTunes
Most watched movie	*The Empire Strikes Back*
Most watched TV show	*Absolutely Fabulous*
Airplane Seat	2A Window
Item	Luggage
Item Size	24 × 64
Luggage Brand	Tumi
Keywords	metadata; luggage; black; Tumi; airline; travel; lost; found

Chapter 2

Metadata: Some Assembly Required

Where is the wisdom we have lost in knowledge? Where is the knowledge we have lost in information?[1]

— T.S. Eliot

2.1 What Is Metadata

If data is the foundation of all knowledge, then metadata is the structure upon which to build meaning and value. A progressive journey that starts with data, then information, onto knowledge, and ending with the pinnacle at wisdom, data is where it all begins, and the meaning of each and every element of that data serves as the knowledge foundation. It is the data about the data—the metadata—that makes the difference. It is meaningful and necessary for data to be identified, described, and discovered. But metadata is more than just the data about data, it is the essence of your content, and it's time to proclaim its importance in business, marketing operations, creative asset production, and distribution.

An *asset* is any form of digital content and/or media that has been formatted into a binary source and includes the right to use it.[2] A digital file without the

---

[1] T.S. Eliot quote. https://quotepark.com/quotes/1015080-ts-eliot-where-is-the-wisdom -we-have-lost-in-knowledge-whe/

[2] *Web Style Guide & Best Practices.* University of Missouri–St Louis (UMSL). http:// www.umsl.edu/marketing/web/styleguide.html

right to use it is not an asset. Types of digital assets include, but are not limited to, the following: product images, photography, logos, illustrations, animations, audio and video clips, presentations, MS Office documents and spreadsheets, CAD files, 3D files, etc. In marketing and creative services, the word *content* is often seen as both the information and the experiences that are directed toward the audience/consumers. This could be audio, video, textual, or interactive. You cannot have content without assets, information, and experiences. Each is unique and has meaning and value in its origin, use, and reuse.

Metadata is a *strategic* imperative for any organization looking to manage and exploit its knowledge more effectively. Metadata is the spirit of an intellectual or creative asset . . . it's everything you have. In its purest form, metadata is information that describes other data—it is data about data. Metadata, both in a singular form and as a collective, is the nature of content[3]—the descriptive, administrative, and structural data[4] that defines your assets.

1. **Descriptive** metadata describes an asset, an object, an item for discovery and identification as you would do in a search on Google® or any other search tool. It includes elements such as title, creator, author, and keywords.
2. **Structural** metadata indicates how compound objects are put together— for example, how a digital image is configured as provided in Exchangeable Image File (EXIF) data, or how pages are ordered to form chapters (e.g., file format, file dimension, and file length).[5]
3. **Administrative** metadata provides information that helps manage an asset. Two common subsets of administrative data are *rights management* metadata, which deals with intellectual property rights, and *preservation* metadata, which contains information needed to archive and preserve a resource.

---

[3] The definition of content itself is worthy of discussion, and Edward Snowden provides an extraordinary example in his biography *Permanent Record* with the following, "[C]ontent is usually defined as something that you knowingly produce. You know what you're saying during a phone call, or what you're writing in an email. But you have hardly any control over the metadata you produce because it is generated automatically. Just as it's collected, stored, and analyzed by a machine, it's made by machine, too, without your participation or even consent. Your devices are constantly communicating for you whether you want them to or not. And, unlike the humans you communicate with of your own volition, your devices don't withhold private information or use code words in an attempt to be discreet. They merely ping the nearest cell phone towers with signals that never lie." p. 180.

[4] Inspired by Riley, J. (n.d.). Understanding metadata. What is metadata, and what is it for? *A Primer Publication of the National Information Standards Organization.* https://groups .niso.org/apps/group_public/download.php/17446/Understanding%20Metadata.pdf

[5] Ellyard, P. (blog). (2018, August 28). Rethinking content management. Ellyard Enterprises. https://www.documentmanagementsoftware.com.au/rethinking-content-management/

Table 2.1 Dublin Core® Metadata Element Set

1	Contributor	An entity responsible for making contributions to the resource
2	Coverage	The spatial or temporal topic of the resource, the spatial applicability of the resource, or the jurisdiction under which the resource is relevant
3	Creator	An entity primarily responsible for making the resource
4	Date	A point or period of time associated with an event in the life cycle of the resource
5	Description	An account of the resource
6	Format	The file format, physical medium, or dimensions of the resource
7	Identifier	An unambiguous reference to the resource within a given context
8	Language	A language of the resource
9	Publisher	An entity responsible for making the resource available
10	Relation	A related resource
11	Rights	Information about rights held in and over the resource
12	Source	A related resource from which the described resource is derived
13	Subject	The topic of the resource
14	Title	A name given to the resource
15	Type	The nature or genre of the resource

One of the best places to start working on your metadata is to consider the *Dublin Core® Metadata Element Set*,[6] originating during the 1995 invitational OCLC/NCSA Metadata Workshop.[7] The resources described using the Dublin Core may be a variety of digital resources such as videos, images, and web pages, as well as physical resources such as books or CDs, and objects such as artworks. These digital resources, or assets, are common in the ideation, creation, use, and distribution by all organizations and businesses working in content (see Table 2.1).

---

[6] Dublin Core. WordDisk. https://worddisk.com/wiki/Dublin_Core/

[7] The OCLC, known at that time as the Online Computer Library Center—a library consortium based in Dublin, Ohio—and the NCSA (National Center for Supercomputing Applications). This 15-element Dublin Core (also known as the Dublin Core Metadata Element Set) has been formally standardized as ISO 15836, ANSI/NISO Z39.85, and IETF RFC 5013. The core properties are part of a larger set of DCMI Metadata Terms. Dublin Core metadata may be used for multiple purposes, from simple resource description, to combining metadata vocabularies of different metadata standards, to providing interoperability for metadata vocabularies in the linked data cloud and Semantic Web implementations.

Metadata Model example

Descriptive	Form of Entry	Status	Format	Field Length	Value / CV	System of Record	Definition
1 Description	Manual	Required	Text	250 chars	Manual	DAM	An account of the content of the item. This is to be in brief narrative form and describing the key areas of interest of the item.
2 Date - Creation	Manual	Required	Date	250 chars	Manual	DAM	Date of creation of the original resource.
3 Date - Release	Manual	Required	Date	250 chars	Manual	DAM	Date of asset publication for internal and/or external use in the live DAM system.
4 Date - Expiration	Manual	Optional	Date	250 chars	Manual	DAM	Date of expiration within the live DAM system.
5 Content Type	Drop Down	Required	Drop down	250 chars	from CV	DAM	Assets categorized in their business relevant context.
6 Audience	Drop Down	Required	Drop down	250 chars	from CV	DAM	Intended audience for use.
7 Channel (Media)	Drop Down	Required	Drop down	250 chars	from CV	DAM	Media used to deliver the information.
8 Language	Drop Down	Required	Drop down	250 chars	from CV	DAM	Primary language of the asset.
9 Keywords	Manual	Required	Text	250 chars	Manual	DAM	Keywords that describe the topic.
10 Creator	Manual	Required	Text	250 chars	Manual	DAM	Primary individual or entity responsible for the creation of the asset.
11 Location	Manual	Required	Text	250 chars	Manual	DAM	Primary location of the asset
12 Asset Title	Manual	Required	Alpha Numeric	250 chars	Manual	DAM	Primary and original name associated with the asset
13 Source / Business Unit	Manual	Required	Alpha Numeric	250 chars	Manual	DAM	Primary source of the asset within the business or organization

Technical

	Form of Entry	Status	Format	Field Length	Value / CV	System of Record	Definition
14 File Format	Automatic	Required	Text	250 chars	Automatic	DAM	Format for the asset (jpg, gif, eps, psd, etc.)
15 File Dimension	Automatic	Required	Numeric	250 chars	Automatic	DAM	Physical dimensions of the asset (1072 x 890)
16 File Resolution	Automatic	Required	Numeric	250 chars	Automatic	DAM	Measurement for the sharpness and clarity of an image
17 File Size	Automatic	Required	Numeric	250 chars	Automatic	DAM	Size of the asset in the system (e.g. 260 MB)
18 File Length	Automatic	Required	Numeric	250 chars	Automatic	DAM	Length of the asset in the system (e.g. 45 seconds)
19 File Type	Manual	Required	Drop down	250 chars	from CV	DAM	Based on mime-type (regular, directory, special)
20 File Name	Automatic	Required	Text	250 chars	Automatic	DAM	File Name. Name given to the asset based on subject with user in mind.
21 Date Updated	Automatic	Required	Date	250 chars	Automatic	DAM	Last date the asset was modified
22 Date Added	Automatic	Required	Date	250 chars	Automatic	DAM	Date of adding asset to the live DAM system.

Administrative

	Form of Entry	Status	Format	Field Length	Value / CV	System of Record	Definition
23 Rights	Manual	Required	Text	250 chars	Manual	DAM	Information about the rights held in and over the asset
24 Contact Information	Manual	Required	Text	250 chars	Manual	DAM	Primary contact name / role / team / agency for the asset
25 Agency Information	Manual	Required	Text	250 chars	Manual	DAM	Primary contact name / role / team / agency for the asset
26 Notes	Manual	Optional	Text	250 chars	Manual	DAM	An account of the content of the resource
27 Asset ID	Automatic	Required	Numeric	250 chars	Automatic	DAM	The system generated ID associated to an individual and specific asset

Figure 2.1 A Metadata Model Example

The power of what the Dublin Core brought to business and popular discourse is the discipline upon which to identify and describe what was then understood as *multi-media* or *dynamic* assets.

Throughout my academic and professional career, I have seen many metadata models/schema used in many different industries for many different purposes. Choosing the right fields for the right content is not always easy, and it is good to have a guide. (See Figures 2.1 and 2.2.)

	Top Metadata Fields
	Descriptive
1	Asset Title
2	Creator
3	Date - Creation
4	Description
5	Keywords
6	Channel
7	Location
8	Language
9	Source / Business Unit
	Technical / Structural
10	File Name
11	File Size
12	File Type
13	File Format
14	File Length
	Administrative
15	Asset ID
16	Rights Information / Copyright / Licensing

Figure 2.2   Top Metadata Model Fields

Metadata fields are the primary elements that will be applied to a piece of data to provide additional information about it. Fields are populated by values, which can be free-form text, controlled vocabularies, or radio buttons.

A metadata value is the actual piece of information that describes the piece of data. It can be selected from a drop-down list or filled in free-form.

Filters are used to define a search experience; filters are applied to a set of search results to narrow down the pool of results from a more general, larger pool to a more specific set of assets.

As an example, if you are an eCommerce user looking for a set of commonly used packaging shots and their associated assets:

- ▪ Some valuable metadata to show in the UX may include the Product ID, the Bar Code, UPC, or even the Trade SKU #.

Another example: if you are a marketing user looking for a set of commonly used campaign assets:

- ▪ Some valuable metadata to show is the Campaign Name for marketers and subsequently the assets they work with.

2.2 Metadata Standards

A standard is an agreed level of quality used as a measure or norm in comparative evaluations. It needs to be evaluated on a regular basis through the ongoing work of the metadata manager/taxonomist. If you are in a specific industry that warrants such use, then it is good to follow through and use an industry standard if you can find one that applies and extend it as needed; created by industry members to meet the specific needs of that industry; standards adoption results in huge cost savings. Some common standards in use today:

- • Dublin Core
- • ONIX
- • SMPTE
- • PRISM®
- • METS and MODS
- • XMP®
- • MARC
- • IPTC

Which one(s) you use depends on the business purpose(s) you want to accomplish.

Regarding standards, never miss the opportunity to learn more about some of the available metadata standards specific to your industry or application. Consider participating in the standards community by publishing your updates with the governing body.

2.2.1 Metadata Storage

Metadata may well be found inside the content file itself in the file headers, file properties, and even the XMP®[8] associated with your asset. The metadata may also be held somewhere separate, such as in a digital asset management (DAM) system or a content management system (CMS), and possibly as a separate metadata database. Wherever it may be, there are ongoing storage issues associated with metadata, including, most notably, losing the metadata in migrations from one application to another. Unfortunately, metadata may become separated when content is moved, which is why migration efforts must be tightly managed before any content is moved. If you lose the metadata, you lose it all and its associated history. The same metadata may need to apply to multiple files in a workflow. Consistent in-file metadata will be impossible if you copy files and modify them. Whatever your unique situation might be, you must maintain the metadata.

Inside the content file itself are:

- Headers,[9] file properties, XMP packets.
- In your DAM or CMS or other content management system.
- In a separate metadata database.
- Storage issues:
  - ○ Applications lose existing metadata.
  - ○ Metadata may become separated when content is moved.
  - ○ The same metadata may need to apply to multiple files in a workflow.
  - ○ If you make copies of files and modify them, consistent in-file metadata will be impossible.
  - ○ You MUST maintain the metadata.

---

[8] The Extensible Metadata Platform (XMP) is an ISO standard, originally created by Adobe Systems Inc., for the creation, processing, and interchange of standardized and custom metadata for digital documents and data sets. It provides guidelines for embedding XMP information into popular image, video, and document file formats, such as jpeg and PDF, without breaking their readability by applications that do not support XMP. Therefore, the non-XMP metadata has to be reconciled with the XMP properties. Although metadata can alternatively be stored in a sidecar file, embedding metadata avoids problems that occur when metadata is stored separately. The XMP data model, serialization format, and core properties is published by the International Organization for Standardization (ISO®) as ISO 16684-1:2012 standard.

[9] Smull, S. (n.d.). Hidden content in your documents: What you don't know can be dangerous. *Corporate Council Business Journal.* https://ccbjournal.com/articles/hidden -content-your-documents-what-you-dont-know-can-be-dangerous? (A great article outlining the hidden information in documents thanks to the metadata and including many high-profile examples of legal scenarios in which metadata caused problems.)

And yet, metadata is an asset unto itself—and an important one, at that. It provides the foundation and structure needed to make your assets more discoverable, accessible, and, therefore, more valuable. In other words, metadata makes them *smart assets*. Simply digitizing video, audio, graphic files, and more only scratches the surface of their value as digital assets. Their full potential is realized only by their use, and they can only be used if they can be found. The robustness and relevance of the metadata associated with an asset is what makes it findable and therefore usable.

2.3 Related Metadata Concepts

A *controlled vocabulary* is used in drop-down pick lists, and the use of preferred terms is a good way to provide authority and consistency to your digital assets. Each tag could point to a different topic, but fundamentally it's the same principal element of the subject under review that is relevant. If the topic is "country" and you only have eight countries with which you work, then those eight countries are comprised by your controlled list. Control and, stronger yet, authority, is needed to describe your assets. *You need to know what it is you are describing and how it may best be described.*

Structured data refers to information with a good level of control and organization—for example, a "date" value in an "expiration date" field. Structured data is usually found in a controlled data environment with inherent meaning and purpose. *Unstructured data* lacks that control and meaning; it offers a confused sense of purpose and requires analysis or interpretation to restore meaning. Using the example above, if a "date" is discovered with no "field" in which to provide that control and structure, what does that tell you? The interest is in wrangling all that data to create a more structured sense of purpose for the content in your organization; it makes information more relevant, palpable, understandable, and usable.

2.3.1 Control and Consistency

Consistency is important. Consider the following tags:

- President Barack Obama
- Barack Obama
- President Obama
- Obama

Each tag could point to a different topic. Yet, fundamentally, it's the same principal element of the subject of "President Barack Obama" that is relevant. *Control,* and stronger yet, *authority,* is needed to describe your assets. You need to know *what it is you are describing and how it may best be described.*

A controlled vocabulary for your drop-downs/pick lists, the use of preferred terms, and the use of synonyms are all good ways in which to take control and provide authority and consistency to your assets (see Figure 2.3).

Figure 2.3   Synonym Ring Cat . . . or Is It a Kitten? (*Source:* https://coolwall papers.me/3076619-adorable_animal_cat_cute_furry_kitten_kitty_little_mammal _pet_portrait.html)

2.4 Key Findings Across Industries and Clients

Throughout my career, I have worked with clients across many industries, including media and entertainment, health, insurance, consumer packaged goods (CPG), retail, and pharmaceuticals, to help them with digital strategy and information management. Over time, we have discovered common themes among metadata and digital problems:

- Little or no metadata planning for new process or systems
- No clear ownership over digital assets and their management
- No current documentation on metadata/controlled vocabulary
- Lack of documentation and control over assets

- Poor labeling of folders and assets
- Agencies, such as external advertising or digital agencies, that are often the default single source of truth

Metadata serves the same functions in asset discovery as good cataloging does by:

1. Allowing assets to be found by relevant criteria
2. Identifying assets
3. Bringing similar assets together
4. Distinguishing dissimilar assets
5. Giving location information

Metadata matters and needs to be addressed at the beginning of any content strategy, not at the end of the business requirements gathering process. It is worthy of concern for any practice looking to manage digital assets effectively within an organization.

2.4.1 Metadata Value

According to recent research, almost 25 percent of time is wasted searching for existing assets and recreating them when they aren't found.[10] This can become very expensive in lost productivity and frustration in nondiscovery. The key is good metadata—your content wants to be found.

Make Machines Smart—Automate Processes

- Content identification, reuse, and management
- Workflow automation
- Automated distribution

Rights Management, Licensing, and Compliance

- Rights tracking, enforcement, and compliance—more effective rights enforcement resulting in stronger revenue retention

---

[10] Chui, M., Manyika, J., Bughin, J. et al. (2012). The social economy: Unlocking value and productivity through social technologies. McKinsey Global Institute. https://www.mckinsey.com/industries/technology-media-and-telecommunications /our-insights/the-social-economy

2.4.2 A Necessary Defense

Metadata is the best way to protect yourself and to defend your digital assets from information anxiety and mismanagement. The struggle is managing within a big-data landscape, in which the data is as complex as the digital workflows it supports. This landscape may include not only your internal one, but also the wider geography of your partners and third-party entities that crawl for your data on the very public internet. Add to data complexity the increasing rate at which it is produced and the diversity of the formats being used. You know that your assets are critical to your business operations, and you want them to be discovered at all points within a digital life cycle, from creation to discovery and distribution.[11] To accomplish this, you need a discernible sense of trust and certainty that your data is accurate and usable. Metadata matters and is not only your best chance for a return on investment on the assets you have created but also a line of defense against lost opportunities. Think about the digital experience for your users and ensure they identify, discover, and experience *your brand* the way in which it was intended. It is a necessary defense.

2.5 Metadata Design: Where to Start?

The path to good metadata design begins with the realization that your digital assets need to be identified, organized, and made available for discovery. The following questions serve as the beginning of that design:

1. *What problems do you need to solve?*
   Ensure that you know the business goals of your organization and how metadata may contribute to those goals. The goal is to be *cohesive* and not disjointed.
2. *Who is going to use the metadata and for what?*
   Determine who is the audience for the metadata, and consider how much metadata you need; the best strategy is accurate intelligence.
3. *What kinds of metadata are important for those purposes?*
   Metadata may well be expensive; make your model extensible, and allow for its natural growth and evolution over time.

---

[11] Ellyard, P. (blog). (2018, August 28). Rethinking content management. Ellyard Enterprises. https://www.documentmanagementsoftware.com.au/rethinking-content-management/

Metadata is the foundation for your digital strategy. It is needed to deliver an optimized and fully engaging consumer experience. There are other critical steps to take, including building the right team, making the correct business case, and performing effective requirements gathering—but nothing can replace an effective metadata foundation for your digital strategy. As previously stated, you want your assets to be discovered, and they want to be found. Content may still be queen, but the user is also worthy, because if you have great content and no one can find it, the value of the content is no better than if it did not exist.[12] Metadata will help ensure that you are building the right system for the right users.

In order for metadata to become truly powerful, it needs to be adopted by the business as critical to operations, marketing, and IT. In order to find something, you need to know what you are looking for. And, in order to know how to find what you are looking for, you need to know what is important to you, to become what is important in what you find. The process appears to be easy, and while search and discovery are part of the identification process, more needs to be done. The following best practices are a great place to start.

2.5.1 Metadata Best Practices

- *Start with a few elements that apply to all and gradually add division-specific, then group-specific standards.* You want to start small and be focused, whether it be one group of assets, a division within the company, or an asset class. Don't over-engineer. Start simple and add if required. First find that success, and then expand that to the next level or grouping.
- *Attend workshops with subject matter experts (SMEs) and stakeholders to gain additional understanding of content, including SME analysis of content.* Time spent with those working with your assets, from ideation, to creation, to review and approval, to distribution is always a good thing to do.
- *Holding card-sorting exercises with business customers or end users to determine intuitive clustering and category names is one approach.* Having your content and all associated words used in description and classification helps focus on what is important and what the priorities are as you describe and find your content.
- *Be aware of the competition and how they name/categorize products.* No one is ever truly alone in the work of metadata, and the opportunity to investigate what other organizations, brands, or services are doing may well

---

[12] Windsor, R. (2014). Metadata whitepaper from Optimity Advisors. DAM News. https://digitalassetmanagementnews.org/taxonomy-metadata/metadata-whitepaper-from-optimity-advisors/

provide new insight and a fresh perspective on how others are managing their content. The internet is home to all your competitors, so use it to your advantage.

- *Be aware of cultural and political points of view.* For many organizations, the audience upon which content is distributed is global in nature, encompassing different regions of the world, languages, social norms, religious beliefs, and political sensibilities. A word or a practice in one country may well be different in another, and yet the content may be the same—for instance, the North American understanding of a "french fry" versus the UK understanding of a "chip." Similarly, the "potato chip" in North America and the "crisp" in the UK. This is where the power of good governance comes into play (which is discussed in a future chapter) and the ability to manage respectful decisions on the application of metadata to your content.

- *Metadata is a program, NOT a project.* By definition, a project has a start date and an end date. This is not true for metadata, as it goes well beyond a project stage to allow for change, additions, and evolution over time, as products and services are added, as language evolves, and the priorities upon which to access information change. The goal is to achieve metadata maturity in stages with feedback loops, user testing, and evaluations.

- *Content is no longer queen; the user is also worthy.* While it is critical to have content to distribute to your audience, it is worthless if your users do not know how to find it, let alone interact with it. Always take the time to understand who your users are; work with them in the planning and development stages, as well as after completion, and ongoing so as to elicit their feedback and ensure the content is accessible and meaningful to them. Ensure that you are building the right system for the right users.

- *Metadata creates a competitive advantage.* The better your content is organized with good metadata, the more efficiently it will be found by your users, to be used and reused in their efforts, ultimately benefiting the business in its short- and long-term efforts.

- *Metadata is a human endeavor.* Metadata is not magic—it requires real effort to make it all happen, and you will need the power of people to make this a reality. You need to start thinking of people as a critical step at the beginning of your metadata work, not an afterthought.

- *UX and UI—how your customers want to interact with content before metadata design.* The ability to have a positive user experience and interaction with the application of metadata with tagging, and then finding that tagged content via search, demands valuable efforts in people, process, and technology.

- *Accept that it won't be perfect.* Metadata is a process upon which change is the constant, and it is truly a snapshot in time, allowing for continuous growth and improvement.
- *Implement good governance.* This is not an option—you need governance in order to ensure the success of your metadata program and the content it serves.

Metadata matters, and it is not a trend or a buzzword—it is a fundamental application of asset management, enabling the creation, discovery, and ultimately distribution and consumption of data and content. Metadata demands attention in effective business solutions. You need to develop and sustain your strategy—from the beginning of the process with the information audit, to the data analysis, and ultimately to the organization of your content for discovery. Stay engaged with your content stewards to ensure that metadata remains current, meaningful, and actionable within the ever-changing digital landscape.

Chapter 3

Taxonomical Tenets

Taxonomy is described sometimes as a science and sometimes as an art,
but really it's a battleground.[1]

— Bill Bryson

3.1 Metadata and Taxonomy

Metadata and taxonomy are the best of classification friends. A taxonomy classifies and organizes information, and metadata describes the information being classified. Think of taxonomy as the big buckets in which you organize things, and metadata as the essential bits and bobs in the buckets. More eloquently, taxonomy is the classification of information into groups or classes that share similar characteristics. It is a way to organize information to best solve a business problem based on user needs by exposing relationships between subjects. A well-designed taxonomy brings business processes into alignment, allowing users to intuitively navigate to the right content. It is required for meaningful information management and critical to effective findability. I like Bryson's quote not only because it is provocative, but also because it made me think about his perceived battle, and I hope you think so as well. In my opinion, the struggle is all about access, which has been the rallying cry of information professionals since the days of Sir Hillary Jenkinson[2] and Melvil Dewey.[3] It's all about access,

---

[1] https://www.goodreads.com/quotes/241936-taxonomy-is-described-sometimes-as-a
-science-and-sometimes-as

[2] https://en.wikipedia.org/wiki/Hilary_Jenkinson

[3] https://en.wikipedia.org/wiki/Melvil_Dewey

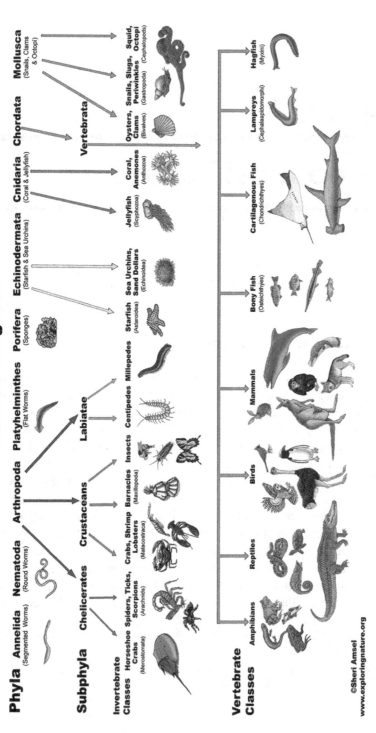

Figure 3.1 The Animal Kingdom Taxonomy Example. (*Source:* © Sheri Amsel, www.exploringnature.org. Used with permission.)

the value of the consumer, and their ability to find the desired content and its associated meaning.

Throughout my career, the following taxonomical tenets maintain their resolve:

- Taxonomies are ubiquitous, but poorly understood.
- Content frequently organizes around naturally occurring hierarchies.
- The overall scheme for organizing information is to solve a business problem based on user needs and to show correlations between subjects.[4]

A good example of a taxonomy is the Animal Kingdom, which is reminiscent of days in grade school (see Figure 3.1).

If you want to see some real evidence of taxonomy in action, then go no further than your local grocery store and walk down the aisles. You have the classic food group essentials—Dairy, Bread, Vegetables/Produce, Meat—and then many different layers of fanciful food organization—Pasta (or Italian in some stores, which begs the questions of what they call that section in Italy . . . spoiler alert, it is indeed identified as Pasta). Gluten-Free, Deli, Snacks, Cheese, Frozen Food, and occasionally taxonomical anomalies such as Ethnic Foods or Exotic Foods, which is incorrect on many levels of ethnic misunderstanding and misinformation. And the usual suspect of Tofu and the food classification dilemma of where it really belongs in the store . . . is it in the Dairy section, or the Vegetable section, or perhaps a Protein section in some grocery stores. As with all good things with taxonomy, what is best for your customers will work best for your level of classification and organization.

Taxonomy may often be seen as an "exactness" for the "aboutness" of an object, a digital asset, a piece of content, or whatever is under evaluation for identification and description. There may well be the absolutism with scientific classification of the very real biological world of plants and animal species, but when it comes to the classification of products and content in a marketing-driven world focused on consumer behavior, the pressure for absolutes gives way to forces such as product placement, priority, and popularity to serve as meaningful points of access. Take for example the grocery store analogy above, and when you are next walking the grocery store aisles, look carefully at where items are being displayed. Some good, some bad, and some are just "other" . . . make sure to always use signs to indicate what is where. (See Figure 3.2.)

---

4 Randle, R. (2020). How to tell if you need a corporate taxonomy. OptimityAdvisors. https://www.optimityadvisors.com/insights/blog-how-to-tell-if-you-need-a-corporate -taxonomy

Figure 3.2   A Poor Taxonomy Example in a Supermarket . . . Where Are All the Labels? (*Source:* Shutterstock, aerial-elevated-view-above-jewel-osco -1249165798)

At an even more granular level of organization, consider the impact of color in product design. Color is data. Color is an essential metadata element in product design both in managing what color it is, how it may be used depending on licensing issues, what colors are being used by similar products, and the ability to search upon color in your content systems. Decisions on color happen early on in product design and continue through the life cycle of products and their associated digital assets and brand management. Indeed, the grocery store and its varied offering of products is a dream case study of taxonomy and metadata. Shopping will never be the same again.

Discovering new information and learning is a valued result. Although that does have value, it must be noted that too much of a good thing does not always yield the benefits intended by the system. If good information does not go into or exist within the system, then the results are inherently compromised; knowledge discovery will have taken place, but not with all the information and content necessary to enact that knowledge. There are many reasons that some content may not be readily available. For instance, unique formats that may not be accessible to search tools; security considerations for specific documents; even the challenges associated with unstructured information assets and their dislocation with structured information in an organization. An effective business case must take this into consideration and establish positive linkages wherever possible within the organization.[5] Sample topics for discussion here include:

1. In terms of taxonomy creation, what type of politics or challenges exists today between groups of owners/subject matter experts?[6] Will they debate and/or argue over terminology, or what should be classified where?
2. Taxonomies must evolve and progress as your business changes if they are to remain relevant. Furthermore, it has been argued that one should validate a taxonomy via user testing. As professional librarians and archivists, are you surprised to see such an emphasis on users and their feedback in order to enact evolution and progress? How common has this been in your professional experiences?

The benefits of having a taxonomy are multifaceted, but the common theme is about *access* and the ability to discover and find content. A taxonomy not only enhances and improves search, it also enables information discovery. It saves resources, as content is classified consistently, and it reduces duplicative efforts. And, as a single and controlled vocabulary within a content system, it enables a

---

[5] Horodyski, J. (2010). A digital asset management curriculum: An information science perspective. https://link.springer.com/article/10.1057/dam.2009.36
[6] Ibid.

consistent search—a reinforcement of "one voice" and the goal of not entering data only once. A well-managed taxonomy also assists in business operations, as it:

1. *Supports standard operating procedure (SOP) and good manufacturing practices (GMP).* It ensures compliance with documented sources of knowledge.
2. *Creates a common language in a controlled vocabulary.* This can be used across departments and/or business units.
3. *Brings processes into alignment.* It reduces waste of time and the burdensome back-and-forth communication with customers and departments.

The business case for taxonomy is one of increasing access to information in your business, an argument well worth making as an investment in your business content.

In order to obtain a better understanding of what a taxonomy may look like, following are two common visualizations:

3.2 Taxonomy—Hierarchical Structure

A hierarchical taxonomy is represented as a tree data structure in a database application. The tree data structure consists of nodes and links (see Figure 3.3).

In a hierarchical taxonomy, a node can have only one parent.[7] It must have content at every level, as empty categories present empty value to users. I recommend doing your best to create a structure four to five levels deep in most cases, as the more layers there are, the more challenging it becomes.

- Have at least two categories for each branch—do not branch for a single category.
- Have sufficient content in each category to warrant existence.
- Balance breadth and depth—taxonomy users must work harder to use a taxonomy three categories broad and nine deep than to use one that is seven wide and two deep.

The problem to solve is one of access and increasing the ability to find content with ease and without confusion. Do you think your users can reach their objective within four or five clicks? More importantly, it is important to know

---

[7] English, B. (2004). The Microsoft SharePoint Community Experts. Understanding taxonomies. Microsoft® Office SharePoint®. https://flylib.com/books/en/2.355.1.73/1/

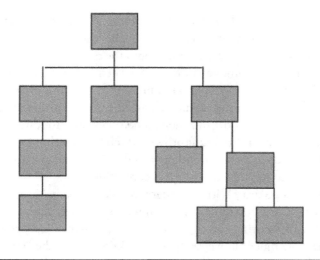

Figure 3.3 Hierarchical Taxonomy Tree Data Structure

who your users are and what their online searching behavioral characteristics are (more on this later in the chapter). There is a difference between online search behavior for personal use at home and use at the office . . . for example, the Google® search on your iPad® from your sofa versus the intranet, SharePoint®, and other shared storage drives accessible from your office. In addition, there is new research showing the difference between the generations, notably the millennials, and their tolerance of time spent and evaluating the sources found.[8]

---

[8] Taylor, A. R. (2021). The information search behavior of the millennial generation. *Information Research, 17*(1). "Members of the millennial generation (born after 1982) have come of age in a society infused with technology and information. It is unclear how they determine the validity of information gathered, or whether or not validity is even a concern. Previous information search models based on mediated searches with different age groups may not adequately describe the search behaviours of this generation. **Method.** The longitudinal study discussed here examined the information behaviour of undergraduate college students who were members of the millennial generation. Data were collected from the students using surveys throughout an information search process as part of an assigned research project. **Results.** Statistically significant findings suggest that millennial generation Web searchers proceed erratically through an information search process, make only a limited attempt to evaluate the quality or validity of information gathered, and may perform some level of 'backfilling' or adding sources to a research project before final submission of the work. **Conclusions.** These findings indicate that the search behaviour of millennial generation searchers may be problematic."

Social technology such as Facebook®, Twitter®, LinkedIn®, Pinterest®, personal blogs, and a variety of other social collaboration tools will plug into the semantic web as data discovery explodes onto the devices used in and out of the workplace, blurring the lines as to how and when business is conducted. Data sharing and collaboration will play an important part in this growth as business rules and policies are created and/or changed in order to maximize the flow of information within an organization to demonstrate innovation.[9] The social enterprise will be a connected enterprise in which social technology and collaboration tools will connect information to individuals and departments within vertical and horizontal lines across the organization.

Despite its popularity within modern vernacular, *search* can be misunderstood by users, as it is too often associated with search engines and not so much on the ability of securing the right information. Furthermore, the question is often asked: how much do we really need to know about the "man behind the curtain," as long as we receive the information we are seeking without too much hassle or headache? It is far more than the inviting and solicitous search box on the screen made famous by the likes of Google and Yahoo!®. The question then becomes how one organizes and structures all these digital assets anyway? Does an effective organizational structure assist in access and retrieval? And why are taxonomies all the rage right now—can librarians and archivists really be that cool? Furthermore, what about the experience of learning and embracing knowledge where it did not exist before? It must be stated that search as a practice and as an active component of accessing information is valuable for its inherent knowledge discovery process.[10]

3.3 Taxonomy—Faceted

A faceted taxonomy is represented as a star data structure. Each node in the star structure is linked to the center focus, and any node can be linked to other nodes in other stars. It appears simple but becomes complex quickly (see Figure 3.4).[11]

The not-so-secret ingredients in a taxonomy contain five key elements:

---

[9] Camarinha-Matos, L., Afsarmanesh, H., Galeano, N., and Molina, A. (2009). Collaborative networked organizations—Concepts and practice in manufacturing enterprises. *Computers & Industrial Engineering, 57*(1):46–60.

[10] Horodyski, J. (2010). A digital asset management curriculum: An information science perspective. https://link.springer.com/article/10.1057/dam.2009.36

[11] Bedford, D. A. D. (2004). Enterprise taxonomies type, integration & design issues. Knowledge Architects. https://documents.pub/document/knowledge-architects.html

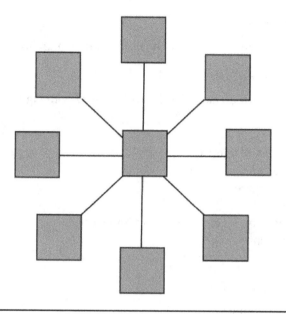

Figure 3.4   Faceted Taxonomy Star Data Structure

---

1 – User Behavior

- Gather both real and imagined:
  - Real: If search logs are available, determine what terms are used most frequently.
  - Imagined: User interviews, personas.
- Survey and interview users:
  - Create a structured interview guide, interview one on one.
  - Use working sessions to dig deeper and get to more meaningful answers.

2 – Curated Content

Acquire examples of high-value content and ask users to produce examples of documents that they believe are critical. You will want to:

Map sources of information

- Map out existing website or intranet.
- Review file shares; document management systems; hard drives.

Look for organizing principles

- Do folder structures make sense? Can they be reused?

Look for currency of content
- Will this content need a new home? (Migrated or archived?)

Is content ownership defined?
- Is it tagged with metadata? Who will know how to tag the content?

Collect terms
- Documents and databases
- Departmental terminology
- Glossaries, indexes
- Web resources
- Search logs (top search terms; basis for favorites)
- Single concept = single term
- Accuracy is everything; specificity is everything

Example—Entities as terms
- Marketing channel
  - Print
  - Audio
  - Online
  - Social media
- Marketing collateral
  - Brochure
  - Media kit
  - Pamphlet

3 – Characterize Audiences
- Who are your audiences and what do they need?
- When your user comes to the site, what are they thinking, and how do they approach their problem?
- Try to deconstruct their thinking process and to understand their line of thought.

4 – Organize Terms
- Look for themes. What are the high-level concepts?
- How are terms related? Are they related by way of process or by concept?

If by process, you may be thinking about navigation. Be aware that you may shift back and forth between organizing conceptually and organizing according to task.

- Define preferred terms and variant terms. Get agreement on what terms will be "official." For example, *SOW* versus *Statement of Work* versus *Work Order,* etc.
- Sort terms into several major categories—logical groups of similar concepts as top terms. Identify core areas and peripheral topics, 10 to 20 to start. Also, consider moving proper names to authority files.
- Result: Loose collection of terms under several main headings. Rough and tentative—see how it fits as you go, then add/modify/delete as needed.

5 – Create Test/Validation

A test draft, or mockup, is an example that is meant to be criticized—this is simply something to use as a reference point. There is no "correct" first pass; allow people to provide feedback and be critical. It is important to review the terms with users and inquire if the terms make sense. Are they useful? Are they descriptive? Are they complete? Are they precise? In addition, take example content (the high-value stuff you asked users for in the content survey) and place it into the "buckets" of the taxonomy. Finally, ask yourself if everything has an appropriate place. What is missing?

3.4 Taxonomy Best Practices

- Reflects the information needs, behavior, tasks, and vocabularies of the users (SMEs and content publishers).
- Reflects multiple points of view and provides multiple paths to information.
- Do NOT enter data twice.
- Not overly complex; it's easy to find needed information . . . users can follow the scent.
- Ensure that vocabulary and concepts are familiar to users.

The best way to plan for future change is to apply an effective layer of governance. A cross-organizational team to develop and maintain the taxonomy core team is made up of core stakeholders from major taxonomy users as well librarians and UX/UI specialists within your business. You will need to know your **Business Context**—the business environment for the taxonomy efforts in terms of business objectives, web applications where taxonomy will be used, corporate culture, past or current taxonomy initiatives, and artifacts within the organization and across the industry. You need to know your **Audience (users)**—the target audience for the taxonomy, user profiles, and user characteristics in terms of information usage patterns.[12] Finally, you need to know your **Content**—the type of information that will be covered by the taxonomy or that the taxonomy will be built upon.

I am a strong believer in both education and the normalization of terminology and concepts that may not be as common or as well known as others. That includes educating your fellow colleagues and, more importantly, educating your clients and their staff on such concepts as metadata, taxonomy, and ontologies. I always include an education section at the beginning of our projects in which we provide a foundation for our work by not just defining these terms and others, but also normalizing them through a variety of educational exercises designed to facilitate learning and increase user adoption. Academically, it is great to see the continuation of formal taxonomy training in library school programs in Canada, the US, and the UK. It is also good to see that other programs such Coursera®, Udemy®, and MOOCs (massive open online courses) also provide offerings in ontology and taxonomy subjects for new learners, and better yet, in a virtual format.

It is also good to consider the ancillary skills that are often required, such as data modeling, SQL, data warehousing, graph databases, and information architecture. I am keen to see many of these subjects, particularly knowledge graph databases, become their own courses and be introduced into established programs such as in information schools and library schools. In addition, what about the technical experience of using taxonomy and ontology tools . . . the earlier these tools can be put into the hands of students in these schools, the better.

My experience has shown that clients in all industries may not know all of what they want, but they do know what they like, may have seen in other places, and would *like* if not *want* a similar experience. I love hearing such things as, "How did they do that?" and more important, "How can we do that too?" It's a process, for sure . . . very much a crawl, walk, run approach.

And you need an effective data foundation in order to do this valuable taxonomical work. Without the classification and organization of the data, you have nothing. It makes it easier to drive everything we will want to do for access to content and information. The battleground in taxonomy development is being waged between consumers and the content they seek. It does not always have to be the absolutes of black and white in order to make it work, but I find the mutable and well-intentioned grays of taxonomy to serve a valuable role in increasing that access to content. That alone serves as good reason to get your content organized so as to not just find what you are looking for but find it through positive and meaningful ways.

---

[12] Galaxy Consulting (blog). (2021). Taxonomy and enterprise content management. https://www.galaxyconsulting.net/blog/taxonomy-and-enterprise-content-management

Chapter 4

Definitions

Dictionary—Opinion expressed as truth in alphabetical order[1]

— John Ralston Saul

It may seem rather peculiar or old-fashioned to include a chapter on definitions in a book, and even more so not as an appendix, but it is in fact of great importance to do so. The world needs more definition and understanding than confusion and misinformation. My observation has been that in too many situations, business or technical terms and their often associated and misguided acronyms are jostled about in meetings, presentations, emails, and documentation as if, from a sense of naïve implicit comprehension, everyone knows what is being discussed.

That may not be so; for some it might be the first time they are hearing or reading these words, and for others it might be an unfortunate continuation of the confusion they have always had by not knowing what is being discussed. It is pertinent to any discussion, business or other, that it be grounded in facts and an understanding of what the subject(s) may be, and providing definitions of terms to your audience is a compelling and persuasive method upon which to socialize the subject(s) and educate your audience.

It is in that spirit that I have assembled many of the words and concepts associated with metadata that are commonly used, to provide a better understanding of the macro environment within which metadata plays a central role. (See Glossary for full list of terms and acronyms.)

---

[1] https://www.brainyquote.com/quotes/john_ralston_saul_404219

Asset

A digital asset is any form of content or media that has been formatted into a binary source and includes the right to use it. A digital file without the right to use it is not an asset. Types of digital assets include, but are not limited to, the following: product images, photography, logos, illustrations, animations, audio or video clips, presentations, office documents and spreadsheets, CAD files, 3D files, and many other examples of assets in use, and even more to be created as new technologies are enacted in the workplace.

CMS (Content Management System)

A CMS is often related to a digital asset management (DAM) system within a business or corporate ecosystem and involves the creation and management of digital content. This is more often used for an enterprise content management (ECM) system or a web content management (WCM) system.

Codec

A codec—a mashup of the words *code* and *decode*—is a program that compresses data to enable faster transmission and decompresses received data. This is most often seen in compression to shrink a large movie file or convert between analog and digital sound: therefore, audio or video codecs. The purpose of a codec is for speed—that is, to speed up downloads.

Controlled Vocabulary

Using a "controlled vocabulary" for your drop-downs/pick lists, the use of "preferred terms" and synonyms are all good ways in which to take control and provide authority and consistency to your assets.

Crosswalk Analysis

A process used to identify and connect various similar or different elements—such as terms in a metadata model—to each other to allow for a better understanding of the subject under review. It enables the connection of these elements for decision making and planning to harmonize the terms in a framework for potential improved use and the enhancement of the access points to the subject.

Data (Unstructured and Structured)

Structured data refers to information with a good level of control and organization—for example, a "date" value in an "expiration date" field. Structured data is usually found in a controlled data environment with inherent meaning and purpose. **Unstructured data** lacks that control and meaning; it offers a confused sense of purpose and requires analysis or interpretation to restore meaning. Using the example above, if a "date" is discovered with no field in which to provide that control and structure, what does that tell you? The interest is in wrangling all that data to create a more structured sense of purpose for the content in your organization; it makes information more relevant, palpable, understandable, and usable.

Data Migration

This is the process of selecting, preparing, extracting, and transforming data and permanently transferring it from one digital storage content system to another. The validation of the migrated data for completeness and accuracy of legacy data within systems is considered part of the migration process. Migration is most common when moving assets and metadata from one DAM to a new DAM or for consolidation or disaster recovery efforts.

DAM (Digital Asset Management)

DAM consists of the management tasks and technological functionality that helps companies organize their media assets such as photographs, video, and marketing assets to strengthen their message or brand. DAM systems inventory, control, and distribute these digital assets for use and reuse in marketing or business operations and help simplify the workflow to ingest, annotate, catalog, store, retrieve, and distribute them. DAM systems may be developed to house different forms of rich media, including audio, image, and video files, organized by descriptive data about the asset.

Dublin Core®

The Dublin Core Schema is a small set of 15 vocabulary terms that may be used to describe digital resources such as videos, images, web components, etc. most often found in a DAM. The Dublin Core most often serves as the "starting point" or "metadata inspiration" for any organization when creating their DAM metadata model or other central data schema.

EXIF (Exchangeable Image File Format)

EXIF is the data created by a camera every time a picture is taken. This can include date, time, camera settings, and possible copyright information. You can also add further metadata to EXIF, such as through photo processing software. EXIF data is a valuable source of "technical metadata" to be used in a DAM.

ERP (Enterprise Resource Planning)

An ERP system is a standard business management application in public and private business to help manage many integrated applications to collect, store, and manage, and interpret data for a variety of business activities and commitments from purchase orders to payroll to sales and accounting.

File Naming Convention

A file naming convention, or simply, a naming convention, is a structured set of guidelines for the creation of standardized file names. The information included in the names of files is intended to describe the primary "aboutness" of the file and may include such pertinent content as date, subject prefix, product ID, SKU, and even location and gender, depending upon the requirements for the business unit and the file creators.

Governance

Governance helps us define the rules of the DAM road, providing a framework to ensure that program goals are met both during implementation and for the future. Ultimately, it is the only way to manage and mitigate risk. Governance can begin with a roadmap and measurement tools to ensure success of implementation during the first iteration and may then grow to become formalized into an operating model for the business.

Linked Data

Linked data refers to a concept by Tim Berners-Lee,[2] the "father of the internet," for a common practice of exposing, sharing, and connecting information and data on the web. This approach is referred to as the *semantic web*. Linked data is a standardized semantic approach to making data inter-relatable so it can group itself with other relevant concepts. Large global organizations and businesses are also using linked data methods for managing and discovering their own wealth of enterprise data.

Keyword

A unique and informative word or concept that is used to describe and indicate a digital asset in a DAM.

---

[2] https://www.w3.org/People/Berners-Lee/

MAM (Media Asset Management)

A MAM system is most often found in the broadcast media market to serve their complex video needs, although it has become increasingly popular in all industries. It focuses on the management of large volumes of high-res and long-form video formats for storage, archiving, and distribution. In many instances, a MAM is often related to a DAM within a business or corporate ecosystem.

MDM (Master Data Management)

MDM is the technical discipline/method of enabling an enterprise (both the business and IT) to link all of its critical data to one file, most often referred to as a *master file*, for centralized governance. In many instances, an MDM is related to a DAM within a business or corporate ecosystem.

Metadata

Metadata is data about data and refers to the descriptive elements that define and describe an asset. It is the spirit of an intellectual or creative asset . . . it's everything you have. Metadata may be broken down into three main categories:

1. **Descriptive metadata** describes a resource for purposes such as discovery and identification (i.e., information you would use in a search). It can include elements such as title, subject, creator, date, location, and keywords.
2. **Structural (technical) metadata** indicates how compound objects are put together (for example, file format, file dimension, file length, size, dimensions, etc.).
3. **Administrative metadata** provides information that helps manage an asset. Two common subsets are *rights management metadata* (which deals with intellectual property rights) and *preservation metadata* (which contains information needed to archive and preserve an asset).

Metadata Standard

A standard is an agreed level of quality used as a measure, or norm, in comparative evaluations. It needs to be evaluated on a regular basis through the ongoing work of the metadata manager/taxonomist. Use an industry standard if you can find one that applies and extend it as needed. Such a standard is created by industry members to meet the specific needs of that industry; standards adoption results in huge cost savings. Examples include Dublin Core, ONIX, SMPTE, PRISM®, METS, MODS, XMP®, MARC, IPTC, JDF. Which one(s) you use depends on the business purpose(s) you want to accomplish.

MIME (Multipurpose Internet Mail Extension)

MIME is an internet standard that extends the **format** of email to support the identification of files on the internet according to their nature and format.[3] This is text in character sets other than ASCII. Non-text attachments are audio, video, images, application programs, etc.

Ontology

Ontology refers to a way to classify and connect items in a more flexible fashion, as it does not need to be limited by the notions of classes and class definitions. It is the representation, formal naming, and definition of categories, properties, and relationships between the concepts, data, and entities that make one, many, or all domains.

PIM (Product Information Management)

A PIM system is a central, single source that manages the content required to market and see products in a corporate and often global enterprise setting. This central set of product data, often multi-geographic and multilingual, can be used to feed data to eCommerce, an enterprise resource planning (ERP) system, or a trading partner. A PIM is often related to a DAM within a business or corporate ecosystem.

Preservation

This term refers to the protection of digital content—assets such as videos, images, documents, etc.—most often in a digital and/or physical archive through activities that minimize deterioration and damage and that prevent loss of informational content. The primary goal of preservation is to prolong the existence of those assets.

Retention Policy/Retention Schedule

Content owners should create a **retention policy** and **retention schedule** that quantifies information or asset life cycle and defines the relevance of a given asset type over time. Identifying what is ephemeral, duplicative, or of low value decreases system burden while allowing the focus to be on preservation of archival, unique, and reusable material.

---

[3] McFarlin, T. (2016). Supporting more MIME types in WordPress. https://tom mcfarlin.com/mime-types-in-wordpress/

Rights Management

The question to be asked here is, "What can we do with the digital assets we have from a legal or intellectual property point of view?" Rights management provides a company with the ability to track the rights for content it owns, for content it has licensed, or for the content it has given to a licensee. There must be serious consideration of any licensing/legal issues associated with your assets, which demands an understanding of what your assets are and knowledge of how they may be used. No technology will purely solve digital rights management; it's up to the business to ask the right questions. The more rights management is based on efficient information flow and integration, the faster and more effective the company will be in protecting and monetizing the content it has sold, bought, or licensed.

Search, Boolean

Boolean search is a type of search allowing users to combine keywords with operators (or modifiers) such as AND, NOT, and OR to further produce more relevant results. For example, a Boolean search could be "apartment" AND "London." This would limit the search results to only those documents containing the two keywords.[4]

Search, Enterprise

Enterprise search is the practice of collecting content items from within an organization's different systems and indexing them in one place for a unified search experience.

Search, Faceted

Faceted search is often offered as an out-of-the-box option in many DAMs. This left-hand navigation for search is so useful for internal searching because it allows users to narrow their search based on key concepts. However, in order for faceted search to be a useful tool, the facets must be built using a custom taxonomy. This way the enterprise, not an algorithm, controls what shows up on the left.

Taxonomy

Taxonomy is the science of classifying information into groups or classes that share similar characteristics. It is a collection of controlled vocabulary terms organized into a hierarchical structure.

---

[4] Beal, V. (2007, updated 2021). What is Boolean search? Webopedia. https://www.webo pedia.com/definitions/boolean-search/

Thesaurus

A *thesaurus* (plural *thesauri* or *thesauruses*) or **synonym dictionary** is a refer-ence work for finding synonyms and sometimes antonyms of words. They are often used by writers to help find the best word to express an idea.[5] The Online Dictionary for Library and Information Science (2005) defines a thesaurus as an alphabetically arranged lexicon of terms comprised by the specialized vocabu-lary of an academic discipline or field of study, showing the logical and semantic relations among terms, particularly a list of subject headings or descriptors used as preferred terms in indexing the literature of the field.[6] Helen Brownson first used this term in the context of information retrieval.[7]

Use Cases

In DAMs and other content systems, a use case is a list of actions or event steps defining the interactions between a role—most often identified by a user or user group—and the system to achieve a specific action or goal. Use cases are most often used when doing the business requirements and discovery for selecting a DAM as well as for regular maintenance of the DAM over time. Use cases may also be used to help with creating the business case for the DAM.

UX/UI (User Experience/User Interface)

UX is generally understood to encompass the breadth of elements that collec-tively influence the experience a person has when navigating and interacting with the DAM. The UI is the series of screens, pages, and visual elements—such as buttons and icons—that the searcher uses to interact with the DAM.

Workflow

The sequence of processes through which a digital asset passes from creation, to production, to distribution. The key to good workflow is understanding the issues involved in identifying, capturing, and ingesting assets within a DAM system and then making them accessible and available for retrieval. *DAM may be understood as a workflow device to assist in the marketing operations critical to your organization's needs.* To determine how a DAM will accommodate your project, it is important to think how and when data is created and modified in your projects, and then think how this data moves through the projects.

---

[5] Thesaurus.world. http://thesaurus.world/

[6] Davis, B. (2021). What do you use a thesaurus for? Mvorganizing.org. https://www.mvorganizing.org/what-do-you-use-a-thesaurus-for/

[7] https://en.wikipedia.org/wiki/Helen_Brownson

Chapter 5

Adjectivity: Language, Meaning, and Optimization for Content Curation and Discovery

The real voyage of discovery consists not in seeking new landscapes, but in having new eyes.[1]

— Marcel Proust

5.1 What Is Adjectivity?

Language is everywhere; meaning is everything; and optimization is everlasting. As we mentioned in Chapter 1, ideally, there is *"a place for everything and everything in its place."* Today, this statement is not only true but an absolute necessity where digital content competes for attention and use within a multichannel distribution framework. To aid the process of content discovery, there needs to be an effective layer of content curation with metadata description wherein content may be managed for specific use and distribution. The practice of this descriptive curation is best applied with metadata—that is, data about data—and, specifically, descriptive metadata. This, in combination with an

---

[1] https://www.goodreads.com/quotes/33702-the-real-voyage-of-discovery-consists-not
-in-seeking-new

adjective—a word that modifies a noun or noun phrase—changes the information given by the noun.

Arguably, both the number of adjectives, their level of specificity, and their semantic value make the effort all worthwhile in elevating the noun to a greater linguistic position and a stronger place of possible discovery and appreciation by the user. In some situations, there may well need to be hyper-specificity, or what I refer to as *adjectivity,* wherein descriptive language is imperative to define specific content. And, in other situations, this content curation is not always a realization of the extremes of hyperbole, or the absolutes of black and white on a spectrum, but more often than not, a gray area in which language has more options for optimization. An inspirational look at content from the perspective of language affects the description and discovery of the objects around us via search and encourages greater interest in the words we use and why.

I am always amazed when the people I meet in presentations, business workshops, and meetings are perplexed and confused about metadata, as if it were a foreign concept or nefarious technological output that had been a burden upon their previous experiences. Metadata is all around us in our work and in our personal lives, to be enjoyed, embraced, and made familiar in our efforts. As content creators and consumers, we organize in order to find something, to make use of something; content demands to be identified and discovered in order to be consumed.

Ultimately, we need to know a few basic elements in order for identification based on the question, "What is it?" This may appear simple by design, but it is not really so simple, as there are many descriptive things to be answered from that question, depending upon what is under identification. Descriptive metadata comprises all those elements that describe something for discovery and identification as you would do in a search on Google® or any other search tool. Some primary examples of descriptive metadata are:

- Title
- Color
- Size
- Shape
- Origin
- Year
- What is it?
- Where is it?
- How was it made?
- Where was it made?
- Why was it made (often found as menu items in the form of attempts to satisfy modern sensibilities to sustainability and environmentally conscious efforts)?

Of all of the three types of metadata, descriptive metadata is the most important because it describes the "aboutness" of the object, or what is under descriptive analysis. It is the first response to a *"Tell me about what you are looking for"* style of questioning or discovery, and it is arguably the easiest type of metadata, as it is the most familiar to us from learning at a young age. For example, an apple may be described as a "red" apple, or a "round" apple, or a "shiny" apple. Just as a cat may be further defined as a "kitty," or a "kitten," in addition to "black" and "fluffy." The basic, simple, forms of description may be taken to a more mature level by expanding to a "meta" level of the original description to varying degrees.

Take for example, the band Depeche Mode, which may follow a descriptive analysis highlighting their musical style as well as their *genre,*[2] a most troublesome word, being the ultimate category in which to describe a work of art to assign it to a category or categories. It is troublesome because the very words used to define a genre are as varied, rich, and everchanging as the subject(s) under review. There is a tacit agreement about popular musical genres, but they are always subject to further analysis and debate. For example:

- Subject: Music
- Name: Depeche Mode
- Genre: Synth pop; new wave; dance-rock; electronic rock; alternative rock[3]

Actress Charlize Theron, in her speech in 2020 honoring Depeche Mode at their induction to the Rock and Roll Hall of Fame[SM], mentions both "rock" and "electronic"[4] as descriptors for the band's music (which mirrors Wikipedia's description), but more could be added to the list, and perhaps the list could even be organized according to a priority order of descriptive terms. Even more fascinating is that these descriptive terms act as a snapshot in time, like metadata itself. The words we use to describe something now may very well be different from what we used to describe them then, and may well be different from what may be used in the future. Language is always changing, and so too are the descriptive terms we use to identify, describe, and access. What was a "new romantic" classification for Depeche Mode in the early 1900s is now "electronic rock," which describes their music currency of the day.

---

[2] genre (ʒɑ̃r) [F. *genre* kind: see gender.] 1. a. Kind; sort; style. b. *spec.* A particular style or category of works of art; esp. a type of literary work characterized by a particular form, style, or purpose. https://www.oed.com/oed2/00093719

[3] https://en.wikipedia.org/wiki/Depeche_Mode

[4] https://variety.com/2020/music/news/charlize-theron-depeche-mode-rock-hall-of-fame-speech-1234825002/

"What's really going to bake your noodle[5]" is that, besides this level of classification targeted at the general consumer, the uniqueness offered with user-generated metadata (UGM) takes this to an entirely different level. Descriptive genre terms such as electronic rock and synth pop will do nothing for a personal playlist in terms of access, but a more personal, meaningful level of classification—such as, "80's music,"[6] or "my fav list," or (even worse, based on my own disdain of the term) "oldies"—will.

Metadata is meaningful, especially when, as you must, you consider the audience. The user, generally speaking, is right, because the way in which users wish to catalog and classify something according to their own schema is the way it works for them. They know what it is, and how to find it, and no one can tell them any different; the metadata self-governance works. This is all the more important to the current younger generation—those "born digital"—who not only interact with such notable social media applications as Spotify®, iTunes®, YouTube®, and TikTok®, which allow for discovery via hashtags or genres, but also then curate that content into an accessible classification system with meaning just for them. This is the concept of a playlist taken to its ultimate level of identification, sharing, and discovery.

We have all been describing content for identification and discovery for years, it's just that we don't call it what it is: metadata. Content curation and music discovery has been with us from the mix tape of the 1980s to the more modern version of the playlist. And for heaven's sake, if you are to align the metadata of an artist or talent with their image to be used in publicity or on other marketing channels, please make sure you get it right and use the right image with the right artist or talent. It's about access. It's about rights. It's about respect.

It's important to remind ourselves that we describe in order to identify and find, and music, like so many other examples, is worthy of such descriptive analysis. We live in a synonymous society in which there are always many ways to describe and identify a thing, an event, a situation, etc. Love the language, appreciate the adjective, deplore any instance of confusion.

---

5   http://scifiquotes.net/quotes/123_Dont-Worry-About-the-Vase
6   An interesting descriptive term in itself, when you consider that a band such as Depeche Mode made music in the 1980s, 1990s, 2000s, 2010s, and hopefully again in the 2020s. The argument can be made that the descriptor of "1980s" rightfully determines the years upon which the band became famous or well recognized, by the masses or in popular culture. And yet this is challenging for different generations discovering music for the first time, appreciating that music, and having to classify it for future identification and access.

5.1.1 The Menu, Please

But is it a pork chop? It's never been just a pork chop, has it? How can it be so? It is so much more than that. It is such defining elements as, "farm raised, grass fed, waste fed, farm name, grade, cut," to name a few. Adjectives such as "foraged" or "harvested" seem rather unnecessary, as they over-emphasize the obvious, but they do make the item on the menu sound more important than it might actually be. A study conducted in 2008 by Brian Wansink,[7] professor of consumer behavior at *Cornell University*, analyzing information from 200 menus and 300 diners, found that menu items listed with descriptive text sell up to 28 percent better than the exact same dishes with plainer descriptions. More is more, and adjectivity works for the consumer and the restaurant by increasing the level of interest, appreciation, and discovery.

At a more granular or specific level, look at a particular food item as an example of good use of language specificity. Pork jowl and pork cheek are two distinct items, close in proximity on the pig's head, but in fact very different, and specificity is needed in order to determine which from which. Similarly, rabbit saddle and rabbit loin are distinct and need proper defining elements. Then there are flatfish: while sole and halibut are common in North America, they are unique and quite different from turbot, which is a more European-based flatfish. Not everything is as similar as we believe, and specificity is a great linguistic friend to have when about to dine. When in doubt at a restaurant, always ask the waiter, or if you're too modest, then simply search the term on your mobile device. Language is supreme; adjectives are essential; access is everything.

Adjectivity makes us want things more because they tell us more descriptive things about the item. One of my favorite coffee shops in the West End of Vancouver, Canada, sells a delicious baked cookie with the auspicious, but not circumlocutory, title of, *Gluten-Free Peanut Butter Banana Chocolate Chip Cookie*. Upon my first reading, I was not sure if it was one or two cookies being described, but to my delight it was singular in nature, and after seven well-chosen adjectives, that grand cookie was defined for me and made available for my consumption. That many adjectives were necessary, if not critical, to the description and required in order to distinguish itself not only from the other cookies, but to those seeking a health-related food-based decision. Adjectivity at its best.

And it's more than just bubbles in the thin glass flute that you are drinking; it's the what and where about those bubbles—because not all bubbles are the same. It's sparkling wine, not Champagne, not because we want it to be, but

[7] Wansink, B., Payne, C. R. (2008). Eating behavior and obesity at Chinese buffets. *Obesity (Silver Spring)*, 16(8):1957–1960. doi: 10.1038/oby.2008.286

because we have to due to historical convention and proper wine classification. Champagne, in fact, is a type of sparkling wine made from three grapes: Pinot Noir, Chardonnay, and Pinot Meunier; more importantly, it is created singularly and exclusively in the Champagne region of France. Proseco is Italian sparkling wine. Cava is Spanish sparkling wine, and yet in Canada and the USA, it is known more accurately as sparkling wine. And, while tasty and popular to drink, a Moscato is not a sparkling wine, but instead is a *frizzante,* which is "lightly" sparkling wine—close, but not close enough to be the real thing.

As another notable and familiar example, look at our cookbooks and the way they are typically structured on a formula based on a traditional model not just of eating, but of entertaining, which often means:

- Appetizers
- Soups
- Salads
- Main dishes
- Sides
- Dessert

However, time has changed our food sensibilities and the way we think about food, eating, and entertaining. Thanks to the influence of a global economy and culture, the increased scientific data of food, as well as new cultural norms and trends, the way in which we acknowledge, identify, describe, and access food has changed. Indeed, many different options for food discovery might now be the norm for many including:

- Vegetables
- Breads
- Brunch
- Cocktails
- Smoothies
- One-bowl meals
- Christmas favorites
- Protein[8]

Although many arguments may exist as to why the diversification and granularity of these subjects may be made, it comes back to the fundamental issues of identification and access to information which drives the change. For all that we do in our business and pleasure, we do so to identify, discover, and access information.

---

[8] Jacobs, D. (2016). *So Many Ways to Organize a Cookbook.* https://diannej.com/2016/so-many-ways-to-organize-a-cookbook/

5.2 A Picture Is Worth a Thousand Words . . . And Yet We Still Have Trouble Naming that Movie

Netflix® has spoiled us in so many ways, none more evident than how movies, television, and documentaries are being organized into their classification system of genres. The latest update shows that Netflix's favorite adjective is "romantic," which appears in 5,272 categories. Following it in order of popularity are:

- Foreign
- Classic
- Dark
- British
- Critically acclaimed
- Suspenseful
- Gritty
- Independent
- Visually striking
- Family
- Violent
- Feel-good

The fun begins when you are able to start playing with the metadata and search for such unique strings as, *Deep Sea Father-and-Son Period Pieces Based on Real Life Set in the Middle East for Kids,* or, *Assassination Bounty-Hunter Secret Society Dramas Based on Books Set in Europe about Fame for Ages 8 to 10.* These titles exist and are found in unique ways, based upon how the user searches for content beyond the regular classification—the most unique for me being *Post-Apocalyptic Comedies About Friendship,* to which there are three actual results:

1. *This Is the End*
2. *The World's End*
3. *Seeking a Friend for the End of World*

Thank you, metadata, for making the world a better place, and for those who work in metadata, like Sherrie Gulmahamad, who tags fulltime at Netflix,[9] making it more meaningful.

---

[9] Grothaus, M. (2018). How I got my dream job of getting paid to watch Netflix. https://www.fastcompany.com/40547557/how-i-got-my-dream-job-of-getting-paid -to-watch-netflix

5.3 Order of the Fittest

We know that words are bigger and stronger than they might appear upon first reading and that not just the word but its placement may well be the key to understanding its message—case in point, the placement and predominance of words used on social media.

A great example of adjectivity on social media is the bio, that carefully curated description of oneself so that *you* know you know but that *everyone else* may now know who you are. This is not the sterile, bureaucratic version of identity found in a passport or a driver's license, but the more creative version for social media, where the rules are few and the opportunities are endless. Whimsical or factual, fanciful or meaningful, the social media bio represents good metadata and adjectivity for the attention users may seek. In 2018, Hillary Rodham Clinton rewrote her Twitter® bio after inspiration from Nigerian-born novelist Chimamanda Ngozi Adichie[10] during an interview.[11] The rewrite went from this:

Hillary Clinton

@HillaryClinton

Wife, mom, grandma, women+kids, advocate, FLOTUS, Senator, SecState, hair icon, pantsuit aficionado, 2016 presidential candidate

to this:

Hillary Clinton

@HillaryClinton

2016 Democratic Nominee, SecState, Senator, hair icon, Mom, Wife, Grandma x2, lawyer, advocate, fan of walks in the woods & standing up for democracy

The term *wife* moved down the list, and *2016 Democratic Nominee* moved up as the top-level classifier. Hair icon moved up a bit, thank goodness, but pantsuit aficionado was removed, and I will never understand why such a metadata travesty occurred. The specifier of "x2" was added to Grandma, which is most accurate for that time, and the more pleasing fan of walks in the woods and standing up for democracy were added to create a whole new Hillary. Or is it?

---

[10] https://en.wikipedia.org/wiki/Chimamanda_Ngozi_Adichie

[11] https://punchng.com/photo-hillary-clinton-accepts-chimamandas-advice-rewrites -twitter-bio/

The person is the same, but the way in which she now appears on Twitter is changed to reflect unique characteristics deemed more relevant than before.

5.4 The Media, the News, and Content Inflammation

Oscar Wilde elegantly, and sardonically, quipped that, *"Conversation about the weather is the last refuge of the unimaginative."*[12] While I do passionately agree with Mr. Wilde on a sardonic level, the very discussion of weather and both its predictions and outcomes is one of pure adjectivity that is newsworthy itself. Is it a snowstorm, or is it a blizzard? And, what a nonevent, if what occurred was what was not predicted. For it was not a blizzard, but rather a bust; not a blizzard at all . . . adjectivity at its worst. Words like *historic* and *life-threatening* are dangerous and damaging, and those in positions of public responsibility and the media have acted irresponsibly. "We received six inches of snow" is nothing to make the snow blower and shovels weep in turmoil. Businesses are closed when they do not need to be. But the attention was heard, read, and received and the point was made—I made you look and notice me.

If data is the language upon which our modern society is built, then metadata is the grammar, the construction of its meaning. Metadata forms the building elements for content that demonstrates meaning for us all. On November 4, 2020, I saw a graphic on a major news outlet listing races of those voting for US president, which caused me to pause and reflect.

Table 5.1 lists the five categories given for "Race."

Table 5.1 Categories of Race in Major News Outlet Graphic

Race
White
Black
Latino
Something else
Asian

"Something else"? This is also seen as "other" or, even worse, "miscellaneous" in many situations. There are many reasons why this is often used, but none are good enough to justify the suggestion of an unextraordinary if not an entirely ambivalent existence. And yet, all they had to do was to include the

---

[12] https://www.brainyquote.com/quotes/oscar_wilde_109875

correct words, as provided by such an authoritative source as the US Census, for "something else," which includes American Indian/Alaska Native, Native Hawaiian/Pacific Islander, and two or more races.

"Something else" or "other" or "miscellaneous" is never appropriate metadata. It is sloppy, unsystematic, and lacks the quality of effort in taking the time to understand the power of words and their meaning not only applied to the categories, and *people*, in our business, but also, more importantly, when seen on such a medium as television or the internet. We need always to strive to do something better, to give value and meaning with every opportunity we have. Indeed, better metadata elements and taxonomies do exist because the content is there for us to use, and we need to make every effort we can to do so. The data is there to provide meaning and authority to what we say, write, and do. So, let's do better.

It is unbelievable to see and read this in 2020, hence my call for all news organizations to *be better* and provide as accurate data as possible, whenever possible. We know what should have been written, so just do it. We all deserve to be seen, be heard, and be identified as who we are. So, no "other" and no "something else"—let us all make an effort to provide the "who" and "what" that gives us "something equal." Metadata provides the foundation and structure to make your assets more discoverable, more accessible, and, therefore, more valuable. In other words: metadata makes them "smart assets." The robustness and relevance of the metadata associated with an asset is what makes it findable, usable, and meaningful.

5.5 On Content

- Value is not found, it is made.
- When one keyword is just not enough.
- We organize so we may discover.

In linguistics, an adjective (abbreviated adj.) is a describing word, the main syntactic role of which is to qualify a noun or noun phrase, giving more information about the object signified. Adjectives are one of the English parts of speech, although they were historically classed together with the nouns.[13] I prefer the term "adjectivity" to describe the current linguistics maelstrom upon which we live in this social media world. I define it as such:

Adjectivity: The over-qualification of nouns, phrases, and even actions, whereby more information, often too much, is given about the object signified.

---

[13] Karima, U. (2017). Adjective—Good Adjectives. https://unijayakarima.blogspot.com /2017/02/adjective-good-adjectives.html

It's not often that a modern-day sitcom entwines a character's speech with sesquipedalian terms such as *jabberwocky, callipygian,* and *prestidigitator.* An example of the power of adjectivity in popular culture was made evident on television with the Canadian comedy "Schitt's Creek."[14] The incredibly flamboyant and irreverent Moira Rose's vocabulary is riddled with erudite, fanciful, and dramatic words, mostly adjectives, to add to her character's incredulity and eccentricity. Only Moira Rose can use such words as, "pettifogging, callipygian, frippet, and unisonous" with such grace and beauty, positioning the arcane with levity so the audience is left smiling even though not always understanding what is meant. The message is clear, if not obvious, for Moira that the bigger the word, the greater the impact, and in this situation, the appreciation of words defining who you are, and what you are all about. The message is well received, and the audience appreciates and applauds the use of words to define this character.

It is estimated that every year, 800 *neologisms* (new words and phrases) are added to the English language. Comparatively little of our modern language is written in stone, for it is always evolving, changing, added to, and sometimes removed from and forgotten. Metadata is a snapshot in time and is also vulnerable to this change. The best way to plan for future change is to apply an effective layer of metadata governance for your content system. There is more to maintaining the metadata than just maintaining the taxonomy and metadata specifications—you must manage the change. Vocabularies must change over time to stay relevant, and processes must be created to manage this change. This is also true for new terminology being added to assets as well as synonyms and/or slang terms and more. Some of my favorites added to our English language lexicon include:

- **Askhole** (*n*): Someone who asks many stupid, pointless, or obnoxious questions
- **Nonversation** (*n*): A completely worthless conversation; small talk
- **Errorist** (*n*): Someone who repeatedly makes mistakes or is always wrong[15]
- **Afterclap** (*n*): The last person who claps after everyone else has stopped[16]

---

14 Wicks, A. (2019). The Bombastic Matriarch of Schitt's Creek. https://www.the atlantic.com/entertainment/archive/2019/03/schitts-creek-moira-roses-bombastic -diction-fashion/584689/

15 Errorist (*n*). Someone who repeatedly makes mistakes or is always wrong. https:// ifunny.co/picture/errorist-n-someone-who-repeatedly-makes-mistakes-or-is-always -SuGgd0ip2

16 Kilbride, W. (2018). Afterclap: WDPD for Everyone, for Ever. https://www.dpconline .org/blog/wdpd/afterclap-wdpd-for-everyone-for-ever

And look at these illustrative examples from the *Indian Express*[17]:

- **Coronacoaster** (*n*): The ups and downs of your mood during the pandemic—e.g., if you're loving lockdown one minute, baking bread and happy as a bug, and the next minute, you are missing the office coffee, drinking vodka at noon, and weeping with anxiety, you're on an emotional coronacoaster.
- **Covidiot** (*n*): A person with their brains in their bum when it comes to COVID-19 safety—e.g., medical tests have proven that, sadly, for the rest of us, no covidiot is asymptomatic.[18]
- **Lockdown** (*n*): A period of complete restriction when everyone's true hair color was revealed—e.g., lockdown was what was needed for a whole bunch of people to learn that "sufficient time home alone" was not the only thing needed to write a great novel.[19]
- **New normal** (*phrase*): What stinks for everyone—e.g., the new normal for this year is to continually get used to a new but much worse normal.[20]
- **Social distancing** (*phrase*) (also referred to as anti-social distancing): Using lockdown as the perfect reason to avoid everyone you don't like—e.g., introverts are desperate for social-distancing rules to be lifted so everyone they live with will leave the house.[21]
- **Zoom** (*n*): The app you use to prove to your boss that you've managed to get out of bed—e.g., has anyone else forgotten they are on a Zoom meeting with the video on and inadvertently started plucking lint out of their belly button? If not, then me neither.

Or, as an example, the new neologisms in 2020[22]:

- COVID-19
- Twindemic
- Anthropause
- Zoombombing

---

[17] Mamgain, V. (2020). New Words from 2020. *The Indian Express*. https://indian express.com/article/express-sunday-eye/new-words-from-2020-7121351/

[18] New Words from 2020. MSN. https://www.msn.com/en-in/lifestyle/smart-living/new -words-from-2020/ar-BB1cfVQZ

[19] Mamgain, V. (2020).

[20] Ibid.

[21] Ibid.

[22] Oxford Languages. https://languages.oup.com/word-of-the-year/2020/

Or, the *frequency rising* of certain words:

- Bubble
- Remotely
- Systemic racism
- Furlough

Or, the actual new words being added:

- **Adorkable** (*adj.*): Unfashionable or socially awkward in a way regarded as appealing or endearing.[23]
- **Adulting** (*n.*): The action or process of becoming, being, or behaving as an adult; (now) esp. the carrying out of the mundane or everyday tasks that are necessary.
- **Crybully** (*n.*): A person who intimidates, harasses, or abuses yet, esp. following resistance or disagreement, claims to be a victim of ill treatment.
- **Fumfer** (*v.*): Intransitive. To mumble, to speak inarticulately or indistinctly; to falter in one's speech.[24]
- **Zhuzh** (*v.*): Style, glamour; a stylish or glamorous appearance or effect. Also: the action or an act of making something more stylish, attractive, or exciting.

Language is organic—always changing, growing, evolving with new words and meanings and uses in business practice and in personal communication. In her book *Because Internet: Understanding the New Rules of Language*, Gretchen McCulloch argues that, "[T]he changeability of language is its strength."[25] Indeed it is changeable; it has to be in order to survive the innovation and speed with which new products and services arise that dominate change in society, culture, and business. We make choices and decisions each and every day on how we communicate with others and use language to shape our ideas and effect meaning to our audience. What we use to communicate and how we use it is a choice in our content curation process and our ability to reach our audience the best way we can. We choose the words we do because of our desired intentions. Our decisions are grounded in our behavior and connected to causes. The rise of adjectivity is not surprising in a world in which fast is the new speed of

---

[23] High IQ Community. https://highiqcommunity.com/adorkable-adj/

[24] https://www.lexico.com/en/definition/fumfer

[25] McCulloch, G. (2019). *Because Internet: Understanding the New Rules of Language.* p. 273. US: Riverhead Books (Penguin); UK: Harvill Secker/Vintage (Random House). https://gretchenmcculloch.com/book/

communications, and our attention is suffering from this effect. We are distracted by the voluminous amount of information targeted at us and always strive for meaning and clarity in our discovery.

5.6 Conclusion

I am glad that language allows for creativity and specificity, as shown in our use of adjectivity, for it doesn't just make things more interesting, it makes us think about the principles of search and discovery and access to information. We consume language via books, online, television, screens, and more, and not only do we want to find what we are looking for, we want to have meaning behind that discovery, and perhaps, even an enjoyable process along the way. Adjectivity makes language and communication much more interesting, and not just because of the hyper-specificity of the words being used, but because it allows for greater meaning in what is being expressed. As much as metadata matters as a descriptive aid, so too does meaning matter to our language comprehension and the opportunity for increased comprehension via language specificity. I love language, in particular the way in which words are used to describe and imbue emotion into their meaning. Metadata matters because language matters in how meaning is expressed in the words being used. Language doesn't always have to be filled with insatiable hyperbole, but when it happens, and the intent is clear, I am forever glad and appreciative that it is.

Chapter 6

Metadata Is a
Human Endeavor

If data is the language upon which our modern society will be built, then metadata will be its grammar, the construction of its meaning, the building for its content, and the ability to understand what data can be for us all.

— John Horodyski

6.1 Metadata Is Not Magic, but It Most Certainly Can Be Magical

Many people may wish it so, but the reality is something quite different. Metadata does not appear by chance or accident. It is not called upon with a daily offering to the content gods we are forced to interact with. It is not purchased at the store, it is not sent by your grandmother in quarterly care packages, and it is not procured through requests sent via letters to a jolly bearded man in the North Pole. Metadata takes work not only to create it, but to also get it affiliated or attached to an asset as that asset moves through a content system from ideation, to creation, to version control, approval, production, and distribution. Metadata is a human endeavor because it takes people power to make it work. Technology helps, and we need it to assist in the process, but humans are essential in making metadata matter and meaningful in all our interaction with content.

Creative professionals and all those working in marketing, communications, operations, and other areas require content be provided as a cost of remaining competitive and delivering what the consumer wants, when and where they want it. Content is only valuable if it can be found, consumed, and shared by your users; metadata is a human endeavor, and librarians are the secret to a successful metadata strategy. Unfortunately, people come and go with very little attempt to curate a culture of documentation, and it is documentation that will save us all in our content conundrums. In fact, authoritative and accurate documentation will aid and abet us all as the threat of disinformation continues to rear its ugly head within the dissemination of information on social media.

A metadata solution involves both technical and human components, most notably the subjective understanding of the rich media assets being used and the creation and application of metadata for those assets. Making metadata work in a DAM, MAM, CMS, or other content system means investing in the construction of a metadata model—a container of descriptive elements about the assets, which enables the user to search for and retrieve the assets needed for their work. There is a certain expectation that problems associated with technology must be solved with technology; though this expectation has merit, it must be a *part* of the solution, not the solution itself. There must be a human component as well in order to support and complement the relationship between the new media (as applied through technology) and the humans using this rich media. I strongly believe that the value of a "real, live" digital asset manager cannot go unnoticed and, more importantly, must be an integral part of the solution.

Knowledge workers spend a great deal of time producing rich information that can be used in one context, at one particular point in time—but then that information becomes lost. DAM users want to find, capture, and categorize that information so it can be reused in different contexts. Those users have to understand and be at ease with the technology, otherwise they will resist change. I believe that part of the job of information professionals is to educate the user base, find out what they want the system to achieve, and help them to gain maximum benefit from it.

Again, grounding those working with metadata, the following discussions are provided:

- Why is metadata important? Is it really just a cool, new buzzword, or does it really make a difference?
- What do you think about automatic metadata? How well does it really work? Will it replace librarians?
- What are your thoughts on standards? Do they help or hinder the process in access to information?

In working with metadata, you will encounter situations in which you must evaluate the costs of developing and managing the metadata to meet your current needs versus that of creating sufficient metadata that can be capitalized upon for future uses. Which one would you choose and why?

And, while there may not be "magic" involved with metadata, there are those who come prewired with the skills involved to foster some magical elements and efforts for your metadata. The value of someone trained in librarianship and information science is that they are the only professional group dedicated to the science and application of managing and classifying recorded information in society. They are focused on the user, their needs, and their experience with information. Librarians manage and classify information in order to provide access; this is as much a part of metadata as it is search and as it is the user experience itself. If you have a DAM, you will need a librarian to help you manage that content and its metadata. DAM involves not only the stewardship of digital assets—their everyday care and feeding, plus their long-term preservation—but also the management of the people and activities that interact with those assets. It also contributes governance that instructs the people and activities around the assets.

The opportunity for content owners, marketing technologists, and all those managing content lies in understanding how assets are positioned at the center of digital operations from creation, through discovery, to distribution. Trained librarians are found in all major cities, and accredited library schools are educating and preparing librarians for work all across the world. It is a glorious thing to witness the clear, comprehensible, and connected work performed by the unsung librarian and information professional. They have helped curate and prepare our digital future with meaning and purpose, eliminating the threat of obscurity and the unknown. If you need a better way and a better future for your content, then find yourself an information professional, and start getting organized the right way.

6.2 What Have You Done for Me Lately? The Experience Needed, and What They Do

A "day in the life" of a metadata librarian may look something like this:

- Drive metadata and taxonomy strategies and approach, with strong consideration to asset retrieval needs and alignment with the business needs.[1]
- Develop and oversee content procedure workflows to ensure useful, relevant workflows that meet business needs across the system and across the asset life cycle (ingest to archive).

---

[1] Jon Paul, Digital Asset & System Manager, Arc'teryx. https://ca.linkedin.com/in/jon-paul-b1995429

- Develop and maintain metadata of shared terms with definitions and rationale.
- Create and improve guidelines for metadata ingestion, including licensing and usage rights.
- Oversee application of keywords, controlled vocabulary, categories, and other identifying tags to assets to improve accessibility.
- Monitor and audit assets to adhere to established governance standards; ensure process standards are being followed for managing assets.
- Develop and maintain user roles and access, set appropriate rights and permissions for all users, and set system policies regarding usage rights in collaboration with the legal department.
- Regularly review the quality of search results to meet user demand for quality access by working directly with users.
- Generate appropriate taxonomy/metadata reports to share with business content owners and governance stewards for regular review and update.
- Provide training and ongoing support on the best practices of content import and metadata application to ensure that all content imported into the system meets business goals and objectives.
- Coordinate and manage all planned enhancements and work with user groups to establish priorities and commitment to planned changes.
- Communicate requirement changes to implementation partners.
- Review and confirm usefulness of system security profiles and user access rights.
- Support workflow oversight and ad hoc change implementation to ensure useful, relevant workflows across the system.

The idea of a "content steward" is one that I have recommended to many organizations struggling with content and metadata issues. Content stewards are needed at all levels of the organization to consider workflow, documentation, and more. A strong culture of content stewardship will go a long way to improving how you manage your information from day to day, with a nod to preserving the past for the future. A content steward will work on behalf of the metadata librarian to ensure workflow(s) are being maintained, to ensure quality control of assets leaving their business units, possibly to take on some of the metadata training initiatives, and to serve as the key metadata contact for their particular business unit. In addition, they make a valuable and natural representative on the metadata governance committee, where much of this work will be reviewed.

The metadata librarian plays a major role in governance and may act as the primary participant, facilitator, and driver of the metadata governance council and operations, and perhaps even a cross-functional DAM. They will ensure continued agreement on the metadata schema, taxonomy, and controlled vocabularies as well as the prioritization of workflow and system changes and improvements.[2] They will be responsible for the development and maintenance of governance policy documentation, facilitating and tracking governance discussions and decisions. They are also responsible for:

6.2.1 Training, Change Management, and Communication Strategy

- Oversee framework and execution of user training activities.
- Oversee the communication and socialization of DAM system capabilities, best practices, and changes.
- Oversee DAM change control processes.

6.2.2 System Upgrades, Metadata Improvements, and Technical Maintenance

- Assist with content system vendor management.
- Coordinate and manage all planned metadata and search enhancements and work with user groups to establish priorities and commitment to planned changes.
- Keep informed of latest changes to DAM system functionalities and roadmap and plan for change in advance.
- Communicate requirement changes to implementation partners.

In the short term, the benefits of a metadata librarian are:

- Users will know how to start organizing their systems and how to best interview users about their needs.
- Assets will be curated to department/team-specific parameters that address department/team-specific needs. Users can track metadata they need because the appropriate fields are available.
- Assets are ingested with useful metadata, or, at the minimum, the metadata that is entered is accurate, and errors are minimized.

In the long term:

- Finding things becomes easier. Users are encouraged and continue using the DAM. Adoption flourishes.

---

[2] Ibid.

- Department and teams become confident in the utility of the DAM and support its usage. DAM initiative strengthens, and data assets mature, as do the resultant insights gathered from them.
- Users find what they need more efficiently. Expired assets are taken off-line, thanks to accurately set expiration dates. DAM productivity is maximized, and DAM storage costs are kept to a minimum, the savings from which the business may allocate elsewhere.

If you don't have a metadata librarian, in the short term, no one knows how to start organizing systems or how to best interview users about needs. In the long term, finding things is not going to be easy. Users become discouraged and stop using the DAM.

So, to summarize,

- With no metadata librarian, your content program timelines will be extended, and there is a high risk of poor user adoption for any content management system. Digital assets will not receive quality metadata tagging = poor search results = expensive time wasted.
- With a metadata librarian, better metadata = better search = better results. Your time is saved and productivity increases; and this is a very good thing.

So do the right thing—get your content connected with those who know how to manage content, and add a little magic to your content.

Chapter 7

Governance

Good governance depends on the ability to take responsibility by both administration as well as people; it has to be pro-people and pro-active. Good governance is putting people at the center of the development process.

— Narendra Modi

7.1 Governance Is No Longer an Option

Governance is the process that holds your organization's data operations together as you seek to become truly data driven, realize the full value of your data and content, and avoid costly missteps. It is a framework to ensure that program goals are met both during implementation and in the future. To be effective, governance must be considered as a holistic corporate objective, establishing policies, procedures, and training for the management of data across the organization and at all levels. Without governance, opportunities to leverage enterprise data, and ultimately your content, to respond to new opportunities may be lost. By developing a project charter, a working committee, and timelines, governance becomes an ongoing practice to deliver ROI, innovation, and sustained success. While technology is important, culture will prevail, for governance is more than just change management—it is the only way to manage and mitigate risk.

The word *governance* is often misunderstood as a set of rules, when in fact it actually refers to practices of organization as well as processes for interaction and decision-making. It does not purport to be over-administrative—either the "heavy" that legislates rules or the "baddie" that imposes ordinances and slows progress. Governance is that unique ability to effect good management and change in an organization, and it may take many forms: a governance council, a monthly meeting, a group of fellow-minded managers trying to make a difference—something to help manage the metadata on an ongoing basis. It is a program, not a project, for a project has a beginning and an end, and metadata does not stop—it keeps going, it evolves, and it matures.

In his autobiography, *Permanent Record,* Edward Snowden argues that "Technology doesn't have a Hippocratic Oath. So many decisions that have been made by technologists in academia, industry, the military, and government since at least the Industrial Revolution have been made on the basis of 'can we,' not 'should we.'"[1] Another example of how a form of governance is needed is reflected in the advice of moving away from the brash work ethic of "move fast and break things," from millennial technobrat and Cambridge Analytica whistleblower Christopher Wylie, who argues for a "building code for the internet" and a "code of ethics"—in essence, regulations to prevent the technological atrocities of the past.[2] Governance is about the ability to enable strategic alignment, to facilitate change, and maintain structure. The best way to plan for change is to apply an effective layer of governance to your program.

7.2 Governance Demands a Cultural Presence and Footprint

A sound information strategy starts with the foundational elements of asset collection, metadata and taxonomy development, and user education. The final and crowning piece of the strategy must be an investment in time and effort into the ongoing governance of all of those elements. This means developing a clear roadmap for review and changes to the assets themselves, the metadata that describes them, and the training materials around them. Governance must manage the change. Over and above change management, it is the process which helps you to ensure that the beginning, middle, and end of your work are not only accomplished, but are managed to allow an ongoing assessment of the health of the work being done.

A good governance model is designed with three major tiers of stakeholders—executive leadership, governance council, system and data users (see Figure 7.1)—with the middle tier being the primary governing body. This

---

[1] Snowden, E. (2019). *Permanent Record,* p. 182. Metropolitan Books. ISBN: 978-125 0237231.

[2] Wylie, C. (2019). *Mindf*ck: Cambridge Analytica and the Plot to Break America.* Epilogue, pp. 255–264. New York: Random House.

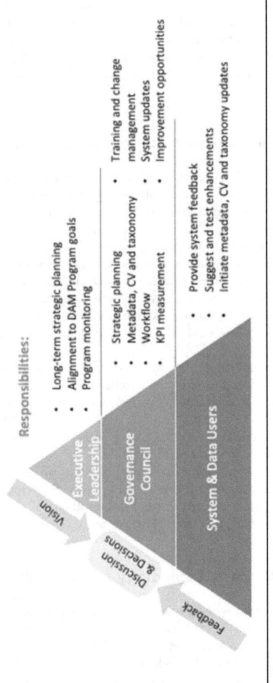

Figure 7.1 Governance Model Example

council is made up of business and IT stakeholders who will act as the primary advocates for ongoing use of the system and metadata. This council is designed to be flexible and modular, breaking off into smaller, focused work groups as needed to accomplish long-term and short-term tasks. As an example, two work groups may be the metadata work group and the systems work group, although additional work groups may be developed as needed to attend to the ongoing needs of system upkeep.

7.2.1 Change Management Governance Responsibilities

Beyond the delivery of an effective ROI, active governance delivers innovation and sustained success by building collaborative opportunities and participation from all levels of the organization, and this is key. The more success you have in getting executives involved in the big decisions, keeping them talking about the content systems and programs, and making this a regular, operational discussion (not just for project approval or yearly budget reviews), the greater the benefits from content and good metadata your organization will have.

We have reached a time in our history when we must implement governance in order to move our content into the future. Governance is the structure around how organizations manage content creation, use, and distribution.

- Governance provides a framework to ensure program goals are met:
  - Managing and mitigating risk in order to sustain ongoing value.
  - Providing a roadmap and measurement tools to ensure success the first time.
- Governance is needed at all stages of operations and at all levels:
  - Planning, deployment, and maintenance.
  - Executive, subject matter experts, operations management.
  - Governance demands a cultural presence and footprint.
  - While technology is important, culture will prevail.
  - It is more than just change management.

7.3 People, Process, Technology . . . and Content

Ultimately, governance is the structure enabling content stewardship, beginning with metadata and workflow strategy, policy development, and technology solutions to serve the creation, use, and distribution of content. Content does not emerge fully formed into the world. It is the product of *people* working with *technology* in the execution of a *process*. Proper governance of information and content must include a detailed review and analysis of all factors involved in their manifestation and life cycles, including organization, workflow, rights, and preservation.

The governance structure establishes the strategic, operational, and technical decision-making process required to ensure that the collective team excels in its mission. Governance provides strategic leadership, establishes priorities and policies, and is accountable and transparent to the organization. In addition, the governance standards should include a core metadata standard, proscribed workflows, and governance practices that will be carried out on an ongoing basis. Lastly, start your governance council sooner rather than later, ensuring that it is a cross-organizational team to develop, maintain, and govern program change.

A metadata schema that includes administrative, descriptive, and structural information allows for data integrity, which equals targeted access, meaning the system will serve more users in many ways. This is important for data consistency and search and is enabled by:

✓ A core set of system-required fields across segments
✓ Segment/brand/asset category fields mandated through policy, training, and audits
✓ File naming conventions and free-form field entry guidelines

Data will only continue to grow. There has never been a more important time to make data a priority and to have a road map for delivering value from it. New platforms provide great opportunities for communication, engagement, and risk management. Data sharing and collaboration will play an important part in growth, as business rules and policies will govern the ability to collect and analyze internal and external data. More importantly, business rules will govern an organization's ability to generate knowledge—and ultimately value. In order to deliver on its promise, data must be delivered consistently, with standard definitions, and organizations must have the ability to reconcile data models from different systems. "Governance in action " (see Figure 7.2) helps create that vision to focus on what to do, and how.

Establishing sound processes and transparency across teams lays the foundation for people and technology to achieve business objectives:

• Cross-functional teams need a common strategic vision and mutual understanding of each other's needs, pain points, and dependencies.
• Engaging teams collectively accelerates solutioning and fosters accountability and ownership.
• Users desire a central location to quickly reference the status of dependent processes and a clear line of sight to ownership and timelines. Transparency speaks volumes. See Figure 7.3 for how governance may enable strategic change, step by step from alignment to structural maintenance.

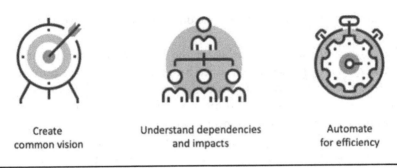

Create   Understand dependencies   Automate
common vision   and impacts   for efficiency

Figure 7.2   Governance in Action

Enable strategic   Facilitate   Maintain
alignment   change   Structure

Figure 7.3   Governance Enables Strategic Change

Good information governance starts with a project charter, a working committee, and a predetermined timeline *at the inception* of any new system implementation or corporate initiative. Although the governance policy may establish rules and measurement tools, the ultimate goal is to create unbreakable, collaborative connections among people, process, technology, and content. Everyone engaged with the content will have a different perspective, so giving voice to diverse views through recurring review and feedback sessions increases engagement and empowers content to work for the entire organization.

Good metadata governance includes the following:

- Adds resources to support metadata strategy and governance.
- Establishes communication channels to obtain end-user feedback for metadata needs and challenges.
- Facilitates strategic planning and decision-making for the metadata strategy.
- Assigns metadata field management ownership to the appropriate information owner.
- Monitors data quality and ongoing value of metadata fields.

- Successfully releases metadata strategy updates.
- Provides communication channels surfacing metadata practices across the organization.
- Provides financial oversight.
- Provides user education and training.
- Fosters communication.
- Monitors DAM system strategy (updates, integration, etc.).
- Analyses workflow.
- Manages vendors.
- Provides system reporting and feedback.
- Manages design and development metadata and taxonomy.
- Oversees onboarding.
- Manages helpdesk.
- Gathers user feedback.

And at a more granular level, it engages in the following:

- *Metadata field administration.* Performs quarterly review of metadata fields whose controlled vocabulary are highly subject to change.
- *Metadata value administration.* Updates fields whose values may change or may not be populated until a later date.
- *Folder administration.* Updates asset folders and may need to occur for archival considerations
- *Stakeholder education and communication:*
  - Partners with department representatives to deliver education for system users.
  - Collaborates with the council to launch education initiatives.
  - Develops and maintains all curriculum and materials and facilitates education sessions.
- *DAM system and program reporting:*
  - Generates and maintains reports on DAM program performance and DAM system usage.
  - Provides summaries of system reports to the governance council and steering committee during periodic meetings.
- *Vendor management:*
  - In partnership with the IT Representatives, manages and works with any DAM technology vendor to implement requested changes and system improvements.

Governance requires participation from all levels of the organization in order to enact real, lasting, and meaningful change.

As introduced in Chapter 6, you may want to consider the content steward, who is responsible for utilizing an organization's governance processes to ensure fitness of the content and metadata. This is a specialist role that incorporates processes, policies, guidelines, and responsibilities for administering an organization's entire data in compliance with policy and/or regulatory obligations, with the overall objective of data quality.[3]

7.4 Best Practices

Management is about execution, coordination, and implementation of results and requires attention to detail as well as follow-up. Applying these management processes to the master information governance strategy provides a structure for stakeholders to both interact with and influence content stored in the system for maximum performance results.

1. **Appoint a governance council.** The council will align processes, requirements, and controls and involve core stakeholders across different departments and varying entitlement levels within an organization. As systems and initiatives evolve, the council can communicate changes and developments across the user base and provide support for new ideas and initiatives.
2. **Assign decision rights and accountability.** Although a collective decision-making process is critical in governance, there must also be an approval process that mitigates the risk of allowing ad hoc or quick fixes to systems or organizational structures. Uncoordinated management over time can destroy structure and lead to costly remediation of problems.
3. **Assemble a stewardship network.** The responsibility to elevate a change to the governance council or implement a change in metadata, for example, can be delegated to a network of stewards who serve as representatives for individual departments. Stewards can facilitate change management for updates, be the conduit for communications, and collect system and user performance metrics.
4. **Anticipate the need for issue resolution.** Engagement from all stakeholders requires confidence that individual ideas will be heard. Formalize change requests for any adjustments to system functionality or initiative strategy. Requests should be formally submitted via change request forms made available to users and, if necessary, subject to review.

---

[3] https://www.coursehero.com/file/p35j9pkn/order-of-restoration-management-updating -personnel-on-the-attack-and-retraining/

5. **Collaborate with IT.** Content management systems within an organization rarely exist in a vacuum. Other systems may interact with CMS, DAM, RM, or KM solutions and offer similar functionality. Involving IT in governance will ensure that content management systems are aligned within the larger technology ecosystem and will also provide support for tasks such as vendor management. Involving IT also provides the opportunity to educate people accustomed to running the machines on the priorities for managing *what's inside* the machine.

6. **Establish communication channels.** The value of maintaining recurring communications with stakeholders cannot be overstated. Schedule regular meetings to hear direct, unfiltered insights and gather feedback from user groups. These often result in innovation and the development of new business opportunities for the system.

7. **Review metadata and taxonomy.** The only constant in business is change, and mechanisms for leveraging metadata terms and taxonomy structures must have the ability to reflect evolving business realities. Beyond checking accuracy and authenticity, consider the effect of database and workflow changes on schemas and taxonomy. Political sensitivities within an organization or changes to the competitive landscape can influence descriptive metadata's relevance. Monitor the effectiveness of search terms in the user interface, and make sure that they contribute to, rather than hinder, navigation. It is also important to document changes to all master metadata governance documentation to make sure specifications are up to date and relevant.

7.5 Why Governance?

Governance facilitates strategic planning and efficient decision-making and builds a common understanding of the content and users' technology. Governance provides a forum for users to advocate for their needs. It establishes clear user feedback and support channels, all the while growing the understanding of required roles and responsibilities. You need governance to both monitor data quality and ongoing value, and to provide a cultural shift to a true system and asset ownership; no small feat, but very much worth the effort. Figure 7.4 outlines the key actionable items of what governance can do in the near and long term, as well as key topics for consideration and discussion.

You, more than anyone, know your assets and what they can do for you. Defining a strong digital strategy demands that you collaborate with those who best know the systems and other resources needed to release your assets' potential. Digital assets are varied and needed for many different reasons in your

Near Term
- ✓ Build common understanding of metadata
- ✓ Facilitate efficient decision making for metadata fields, etc.
- ✓ Provide forum for different teams and unites to advocate for their needs
- ✓ Establish clear user feedback and support channels
- ✓ Understand required roles and representation as program expands

Long Term
- ✓ Formalize and kick off governance activities
- ✓ Support release of content program and metadata updates
- ✓ Monitor governance effectiveness and evolve strategy as needed

Governance Topics
- Metadata strategy and design changes
- Policies and Standards
- User feedback and support
- Training content and execution
- Empowered Librarian to manage forward schedule of change

Figure 7.4 Governance from Near Term to Long Term

transformative strategy. As long as change exists in your business, your strategy will change. It is never really finished. It is important to be prepared for this and to ensure that your solution is flexible and well governed.

Successful collaboration starts by defining what your customers and business want to do with digital assets and then creating the plan to achieve it. After that, communicating how your assets are used to drive business will inspire others, from IT staff to all users present and future who seek to innovate them for future use; it's access in action. Creating a common language and structure for classifying content assets positions the company to maximize investment in content and serve customers' information needs more effectively and efficiently.

Governance is a framework to ensure that program goals are met both during implementation and in the future. As mentioned above, ultimately, it is the only way to manage and mitigate risk. Governance can begin with a roadmap and measurement tools to ensure success of implementation during the first iteration and may then grow to become formalized into an operating model for the business.

Governance helps us define the "rules of the road" as you navigate your way through your DAM, MAM, MDM, PIM, CMS, and any other content-related strategy and program. Managing content is not a temporary measure; it is ongoing, always changing. Governance is all about managing risk and sustaining ongoing value and is needed at all stages of operations and at all levels.

You need to start somewhere, and there is no option with governance—you've got to do it. And, if possible, do it early, even before the DAM is launched. No one is too busy to participate in governance. DAMs are more successful when there is active governance from the very beginning. Make the first move to bring people together to unify them to the DAM, metadata, etc. My experience has shown that there will be a group of people who want to be on the council, ready to start working. Oftentimes, people are recommended as well. In fact, I have not seen much resistance to this, and in fact, management welcomes the participation in governance committees. Any effort that contributes to making things better within the organization is always welcomed.

Chapter 8

Metadata and Workflow

Workflow is understanding your job, understanding your tools,
and then not thinking about it any more.[1]

— Merlin Mann

8.1 Metadata Is Meaningful

Metadata is meaningful because it connects content from creation to consumer. It is able to travel from idea to distribution via the creative workflow, along the way making the content more accessible with each step it takes along its life cycle. *Workflow* is best described as the sequence of processes through which content passes from creation to production, ending with distribution. The key to good workflow is understanding the issues involved in identifying, capturing, and ingesting assets within a DAM system and then making them accessible and available for retrieval.

DAM may be understood as a workflow device to assist in the marketing operations critical to your organization's needs. To determine how a DAM will accommodate your project, it is important to think how and when data is created and modified in your projects, and then think how this data moves through the projects. A DAM system aims to improve workflow efficiency through the automation of tasks such as ingest, metadata creation, and authenticated access. It is critical to not only develop but document your workflow, from ingestion

---

[1] QuoteMaster. https://www.quotemaster.org/q09af37e3571319f32a5e7eb94481bcba

to approval, and even during migration of assets. The key to good workflow is both to understand the issues involved in identifying, capturing, and ingesting content into the system and to make them accessible and available for retrieval.

With multiple touch points along an asset's life cycle, potentially spanning multiple versions and incidents of reuse, a content system can help teams across an organization—from IT staff to all users, past and present, and make coordinated and educated decisions about the strategic use of their digital assets. The unique and distinguishing aspect of a content system such as a DAM is that it can serve as the single source of truth for an organization, preventing unauthorized distribution or confusion about versions. Instead of sitting on shared drives or network locations for which there is no search, no security, and no metadata, a DAM becomes a valuable tool for an organization looking to manage its content and brand more effectively. A DAM ensures that the right asset is being used by the right person(s) at the right time for the right reasons. But it needs metadata-powered workflow to make it work.

Metadata should be populated throughout the workflow and throughout all stages of content creation by those actively doing the creation. Metadata at content creation is best as knowledge of the *what* it is, the *who* it is, the *when* it is, and the *why* it is. It is best understood because it is happening in real time: A graphic artist making a logo. A video producer making an edit to a marketing video. A content writer adding copy to the language on a promotional brochure. These examples all show content creation at the moment it is happening and the ideal place to enter metadata. And it's not always just one person, but many along the way, as that particular piece of content moves along its workflow journey from ideation to distribution and at all stages in between. And, as the content moves along that workflow, there will be different user roles to ensure accuracy and timeliness of asset information; and as it does, the following workflow considerations apply:

- Is there metadata in headers, file systems, naming conventions, query logs that could be extracted automatically?
- Who adds the metadata? Creator(s)? Librarian?
- Will there be checks and balances along the way?
- Does your organization employ automatic classification tools for some or all types of assets? Results are not as accurate as humans can provide, but they are more consistent.
  - Semi-automated is best.
  - Degree of human involvement is a cost/benefit tradeoff.
  - Importance of automated/manual validation processes.

Workflows intersect with content no matter what the life-cycle stage, and understanding the intersections of people and technology unique to each phase is key to ensuring that workflow processes will support, and not hinder, content's smart, efficient utilization. This may well confirm that streamlined, user-friendly workflows are enacted and that they allow necessary process actions to be taken while meeting deadline requirements.

As an overview of how to start thinking about and planning for your metadata workflow, consider how your content is made. In its simplest form, document what content is made and then who is creating it—not just the creator, but those who initiate the content ideation process as well as those who co-create, collaborate, review, approve, edit, distribute, and have some form of touchpoint with the content. Once you have that outlined, then go back and review each of those touchpoints and determine what metadata is being added at each of those steps. Write out the metadata and determine if there is any priority to it and, more important, if any metadata is being repeated along the process. Consider Figure 8.1.

Metadata will occur at various stages of content development in how digital content is made, revised, approved, distributed, stored, accessed, and reinvented. It is possible to identify three broad life-cycle stages that content passes through:

- Work in progress (WIP)
- Final state/live
- Inactive

Each life-cycle phase should be understood according to its defining characteristics, and when designing a phase's workflows, priority should be given to addressing the unique requirements and activities specific to that phase. When thinking workflow, it's easy to zero in on the resources and processes that guide content's work-in-progress (WIP) trajectory—so ask yourself who are the teams and departments, and what are the technology applications, systems, and tools they use to ensure something digital is created, approved, and optimally poised for use. Failure to understand and address process needs according to unique life-cycle requirements will likely introduce a "square-peg/round-hole" scenario that in turn can introduce inefficiencies, compliance risk, and resource waste.

8.2 Administrative Metadata

As outlined in an earlier chapter, administrative metadata provides information that helps manage an asset. While much of this type of metadata may be associated with rights management and preservation, there are some great opportunities to allow for management of your content associated with workflow. Figure 8.2 lists some great administrative metadata field considerations for any content management system.

Integrating Metadata Entry into Workflow

- Enables assets to be available to content system users as soon as possible
- Certain metadata will be tied to specific points in the workflow, based on areas of expertise
- Metadata entry workload can be shared between relevant SME's

Placeholder Assets

- Record that does not yet contain an actual asset
- Useful because whenever metadata is known, content stewards or librarians can add information before asset is ingested

Metadata Templates

- Form that contains fields used in content systems
- Simplifies metadata entry by presenting a small subset of all available fields to the user

Figure 8.1 Making Metadata Work for Workflow

Administrative
Asset Contact Information
Agency Contact Info
Published By
Asset ID
SKU #
Exclusive Rights
Usage Rights
Rights information / Copyright / Licensing
Rights Expiration Date
Comments
Champion
Copyright Information
Rights License Category
Model Information
Model Release Form
Photographer
Stock Vendor
IPTC Copyright URL
IPTC Provider
Import File Location
Import Preview File Location

Figure 8.2 Administrative Metadata Fields Example

Establishing a metadata workflow process for your organization may well offer ideas to make it more efficient or to pursue new business. A mindset that says, "Here is our process, automate it," misses the opportunity to examine the integrity of the process and support future growth. Automating a flawed and cumbersome workflow can be disastrous, and the success of any content system demands rigorous evaluation. In addition, documenting the workflow offers another opportunity to build better relationships with internal teams and partners. The result of this documentation serves as part of the foundation for your content and the people and processes connected along the way.

To determine how the creative workflow will accommodate your process, it is important to think how and when metadata is created and modified in your projects, and then think how this moves through the projects. Your organization's goals may be to deploy a system that will shepherd assets through production and approval workflows, securely distribute assets to global recipients, manage assets through a complicated rights and compliance landscape, eliminate file redundancies and increase asset monetization, or any combination of the above.

8.3 ROI

Metadata increases the return on investment (ROI) of a content system by unlocking the potential to ingest, discover, share, and distribute assets. Every piece of content has the potential to be exploited for a variety of purposes. A well-designed metadata schema also allows automated structural metadata, such as file type and size, to be leveraged to help creative and publishing teams speed the time to market. Metadata is the key that unlocks the commercial potential of information, data, and intellectual or creative assets. For example, by tagging an image with descriptive metadata about gender, marketers can discover and use the asset for targeted marketing or for demographically specific content. A metadata schema that includes administrative information allows for targeted access control, allowing more people to use and search information and content systems without increasing the risk of misuse.

ROI refers to measuring the gain or loss generated on an investment relative to the amount of money invested.[2] This is most often expressed as a percentage and is used for financial decision-making to compare how well the investment performed. Most often, ROI is expressed as a quantitative response, which is a financial number that shows how much was gained or lost due to a calculation determined by the organization. At other times, ROI is expressed as a qualitative response, such as the value or intangible business benefits of such an effort.

Good examples of ROI include:

- Catalogs: ROI based on increased sales through improved
  - Product findability; up-to-the minute changes to advertising and partner cross-sells
- Call center: ROI based on cutting costs through
  - Fewer customer calls due to substantially improved website self-service
  - Faster, more accurate CSR responses through better information access
- Regulatory compliance: ROI based on
  - Avoiding penalties for breaching regulations
  - Following required procedures (e.g., health care claims, archiving procedures)
- Productivity: ROI based on cutting costs through
  - Reduced time re-creating existing materials and reduced storage and backup costs
- Rights enforcement and/or tracking: ROI based on
  - Less loss of revenue due to piracy
  - More revenue due to availability of rights information

---

[2] What is a return on investment (ROI)? https://www.divestopedia.com/definition/1254/return-on-investment-roi

8.4 Metadata Helps with User Adoption

- Clunky out-of-the-box functionality does not always provide a satisfactory user experience, and user-driven meaningful metadata will help.
- if one focuses too much on the technology and not the user, user engagement may wane; users will have poor workflow and will ultimately not find what they are looking for.
- Limited training tailored to specific user roles may not allow for a better understanding of the metadata needed for users to do their work.
- Minimal guidelines and tools to support UX (e.g., metadata ingestion and search cheat sheets) to help the process.
- Do resource gaps exist, such as no librarian or metadata specialist to manage the metadata on a full-time or regular basis?
- Risk of metadata integrity due to lack of tagging guidelines and enforcement.
- Lack of process and communication standards cause workflow pain points.
- Workarounds or existing ways of working to email third parties such as agencies or super-users for assets will be a difficult habit for nonsuper-users to break.

8.5 File Naming Conventions

A file naming convention, or simply, a naming convention, is a structured set of guidelines for the creation of standardized file names. As mentioned previously, the information included in the names of files is intended to describe the primary "aboutness" of the file and may include such pertinent content as date, subject prefix, product ID, SKU, and even location and gender, depending upon the requirements for the business unit and the file creators. It will greatly help you track your files within your business unit and with others using collaborative work methods involving a variety of software applications. If the guidelines are followed, a file naming convention will help you track different versions of a file and determine which is the most current.

A file naming convention assists in the automated workflow for asset ingestion by using the sections and delimiters to support the automatic classification of the digital asset into the content system. Each section is itself a metadata tag that can be applied automatically to the asset and, in some situations, be directed to a specific folder in the taxonomy. The functionality of some systems to parse the unique sections of the file name to auto-populate fields and others to auto-place assets into folders is a great time-saving benefit. It increases the efficiency of asset ingestion and can offer the much needed first effort of metadata application to content. The better the setup with authoritative metadata in

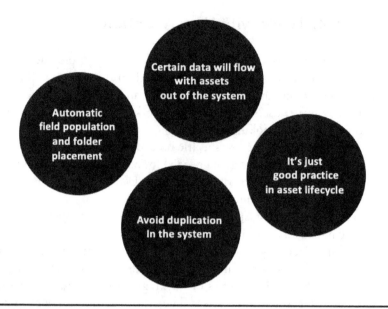

Figure 8.3   Workflow Goodness with Consistency

the file name, the greater the possibility for an easy transition to classification, saving time in workflow.

A good file naming convention will allow for certain data to follow the asset even if that data leaves the system. It also helps avoid issues of duplication when importing digital assets into the system. In many situations, content is created off-line before it is imported into the system, so it is generally good practice to use naming conventions. The most challenging part of naming conventions is enforcement—ensuring file creators follow the guidelines. The key is consistency and good governance over file creation, management, and workflow (see Figure 8.3).

Take this example of a file naming convention for a product image:

Title_BusinessUnit_Date_Counter.FileFormat
WestRegionCampaign_Marketing_20210228_2.pdf

Do's

- Be consistent in how names are developed, especially when using underscores, spaces, or capitals to differentiate between words—for instance, Annual Report vs. Annual_Report vs. AnnualReport.
- Keep the file name short—include only the most salient elements in order of importance.

- When using a date, always enter year first, then month, then day.
  - Month should be in the form of a number.
  - Months and days should include a 0 if a single digit.
- When applying any number to the file name, add a 0 if it is a single digit.
- If using file names to version, be consistent in how you apply it, and always use a version number instead of "draft" or "final."
- Always apply file names with a consistent pattern.
- Article Code and View Code are required, and you can customize the rest of the name.
- Using unique product identifiers in naming conventions, where useful, allows the DAM and PIM integration to automatically apply product data to the asset.

Don'ts

- Use special characters in file names. They might not be usable across system types.
- Use department-specific acronyms or jargon in file name.

SAP Article Code_View Code_ Product Type_Gender_01.filetype
AP5027730_ALPS_JACKET_M_01.tif

Some good rules to remember are:

1. Apply product number or other uniquely identifying numbers first, starting with the most general number and moving to the most specific.
2. If using file names to allow the DAM to parse out metadata, then be sure to use delimiting characters (underscores, dashes) *only* as delimiters for parsing and for no other reason; for example:

Good example:

Marketing_SpringCatalogCoverImage_LifestyleImagery_20210228.2

Bad example:

Marketing_Spring_Catalog_Cover_Image_Lifestyle_Imagery20210228.2

3. Including Asset Type details in the file name helps that information travel with the asset through and out of internal systems. This may prevent misuse with third parties.
4. If third parties are creating assets to be used in the DAM, be sure that they use your prescribed naming convention.

You, above all, know your assets and what they can do for you. Never forget that. A DAM encompasses the management tasks and technological functionality designed to enhance the inventory, control, and distribution of your digital assets. In the majority of situations, digital assets include rich media such as photographs, videos, graphics, logos, or marketing collateral. This is the time to perform a content audit to discover exactly what assets are there, how many there are, and how they interact. For example, perform a content audit to inventory existing sources of content within your organization to document quantity of assets, their source, creators, users, and destinations. This will also be the source for identifying systems of record for assets and/or metadata and guiding the later metadata content audit. In addition, map current-state workflow processes from creation, reuse, or ingest to production and archive and identify processes that can be optimized with the DAM.

A focus on innovative data and metadata use can generate many positive impacts from the DAM or other content management system. Consider the following examples of what powerful effects a DAM with good metadata and workflow management may have on users and the organization as a whole. It will:

- Support strategic organizational initiatives.
- Serve as a resource to gauge changes in customer values.
- Reduce costs.
- Generate new revenue opportunities.
- Provide better brand management.
- Improve collaboration and streamline creative workflow or competitiveness.
- Enable marketing agility and operational excellence.

8.6 Summary

Workflow and governance is the structure around how organizations manage content creation, use, and distribution, and it plays a critical part in developing trust. Ultimately, governance is the structure enabling content stewardship, beginning with metadata and workflow strategy, through policy development, and more, and it provides technology solutions to serve the creation, use, and distribution of content. As mentioned, and it is worth repeating, content does not emerge fully formed into the world. It is the product of people working with technology in the execution of a process—the transparency needed for your content to be successful.

The struggle in managing content within the digital world is as complex as the digital workflows underpinning the efforts. We can build trust through effective metadata and earn trust through good governance—in fact, your

content depends upon it. Creating the whole workflow solution—and connecting it throughout your organizational ecosystem—means that your digital assets can be put to innovative use in generating revenue, increasing efficiencies, and enhancing your ability to meet new and emerging market opportunities. The data-points to monitor and manage in this scenario are actually your metadata and the workflows that they support.

Chapter 9

What Do Good Metadata, UX, and Search Look Like?

People ignore design that ignores people.[1]

— Frank Chimero, Designer

9.1 User Experience

If you want to confuse your audience, then show them a Gantt chart. If you want to demonstrate lucidity and precision, then provide a positive user experience (UX) and user interface (UI) with content. UX is generally understood to encompass the breadth of elements that collectively influence the experience a person has when navigating technology. A positive UX can be the decisive element driving a content system's *end-user adoption*: Users do what the business wants them to do, in the way they are supposed to; assets follow desired and optimal workflow paths; they are enriched by DAM-enabled metadata; and they are findable and therefore monetizable.

Providing robust UX enables users to perform tasks in such a way that the methodology required to execute an action doesn't hinder but rather seamlessly, subtly instructs and complements the experience of completing a task. If something is easy, intuitive, and pleasurable to complete, a user will acclimate to

---

[1] https://humandigital.com/insights/people-ignore-design-that-ignores-people

performing the action with minimal resistance. Without providing a good *experience*, users will not want to use metadata, and not only will failure on that front be a costly mistake in ROI terms, but also poor user adoption will carry additional costs and increased risk for all the objectives any content system aims to achieve:

- Operational efficiency
- Asset findability and monetization
- Asset usage compliance
- Analytics-driven insight into asset use and value

Any business enterprise investing in DAMs, or web content management systems (WCMs), or MAMs, and more, with poor UX is setting itself up for a Sisyphean battle to achieve end-user buy-in and system adoption.

9.2 Search

Search is nothing without metadata as its power. Search is how we navigate data to procure content and, we hope, extract the meaning and value we seek. Search is foundational to digital strategy, whether that be content management or digital asset management. Having everything in place from the start ensures that the project will launch successfully.

The problem with search is that corporate information may contain many types of data, and not all of it is easy to search. So, we need to ensure well-designed UX and UI to provide a fully engaging consumer experience because, regardless of where it comes from and what it is, content drives the DAM and, more importantly, your brand.

Metadata is the constant connection between your content, your people, process, and technology and requires an understanding of how it affects search and UX/UI for delivering a successful customer experience (CX) for your users. Metadata is imperative to search. Enterprise search systems and the search functionality in content systems do not come ready installed with an understanding of internal jargon, terminology, and changes in branding. The good thing is that metadata fills this gap. Successful enterprise search often still requires search refinements, and metadata and taxonomy provide the controlled vocabulary for this navigation, whether faceted or hierarchical. Ensuring that all aspects of an enterprise search project are implemented from the beginning will provide an optimized search experience. In order to get started with this work, a robust content inventory is required to ensure you are prepared. It is important to keep in the mind the following:

- **Content inventory.** Provides insight into the scope of the project as well as documentation of the quality of existing data.
- **Metadata model.** Outlines the key metadata elements that must be in place for documents moving forward.
- **Controlled vocabulary.** Defines the preferred terminology and synonyms to be used to map search queries to the correct content.
- **Search refiners.** Provides the ability to refine search results based on a controlled set of terms and offers specific sets of results for granular topic searching.

The importance of metadata is that it powers the search experience. Good metadata provides good search and is a great example of the common "garbage in, garbage out" scenario in business. The goal should always be to provide the best possible information in the best possible way to users so not only do they find what they are looking for, but also they interact in a positive way, which will ultimately increase the opportunity for enhanced usage and user adoption. Users know what they want and what they do not want, as evidenced by the examples of search in Figure 9.1.

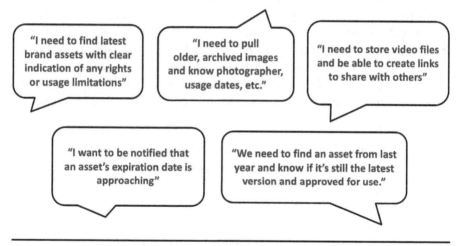

Figure 9.1 Examples of Search Feedback

User experience with search affects the following:

- **Feelings**
  - Frustrated customers
  - Disengaged associates

- ○ Discouraged sales personnel
- ○ Overwhelmed associates

- **Challenges**
  - ○ Harm to brand image
  - ○ Amplified data-quality issues
  - ○ High risk of business disruption
  - ○ Failure in meeting deadlines

- **Inefficiencies**
  - ○ Loss of revenue opportunities
  - ○ Sub-optimal decision-making
  - ○ Repetitive manual data entry
  - ○ Long turnaround of critical processes
  - ○ Wasted time and effort
  - ○ Longer innovation cycles
  - ○ Non-value–added work

Search and retrieval is important because it is directly tied to the principles of access to the content that users are seeking. As we learned earlier, almost 20 percent of users' time is wasted searching for existing assets or recreating them when they aren't found. This is expensive because of costs in lost productivity, let alone the mental anguish and frustration in the non-discovery of content—a non-access event. The key is good metadata—your data wants to be found. My recommendation is to review your current state landscape from the lens of *people, process, and technology* as a way to better understand your UX/UI situation. The following represents an overview of what I have seen over the last 20 years with my clients:

- **People**
  - ○ Misaligned incentives, priorities, and accountability
  - ○ Reliance on tribal knowledge (implicit vs. tacit)
  - ○ Premature assumptions
  - ○ Loosely adhered to upstream deadlines

- **Process**
  - ○ Lack of cross-functional visibility and collaboration
  - ○ Insufficient planning
  - ○ Lack of program/process ownership
  - ○ Infrequent customer feedback loop
  - ○ Complex and inflexible process

- **Technology**
  - ○ Multiple, disparate systems that may not be connected or integrated
  - ○ Lack of automation to assist in metadata creation
  - ○ Poor UX for each and every system

SEARCH
Sort Search
Omnisearch (basic vs. advanced)
Customizable filed sort options

FILTER SEARCH
Basic and Advanced filter options
On / Off filter toggle
Permission / access to search
Admin POV (point of view)

SAVE SEARCH
Is the save search able to be made public? Admin control of saved search? End-user shareable?

ADMIN CONTROL
Can admin control what fields are controlled (e.g. data search uploaded vs created / how ranking and relevance are defined - title > keyword

NAVIGATION THROUGH SEARCH RESULTS
Ability to move from one asset details page to another without going back to the initial search

GENERAL
Boolean operators, wildcards, and special characters, autocomplete suggestions
Title view, list view, page results - how results are viewable

Figure 9.2 Different Types of Search Functionality in DAM

(A description of Figure 9.2 can be found on the following page.)

The triumvirate of people, process, and technology must become a primary principle of your methodology when doing metadata design and development, especially considering UX/UI. The "design" of search is important for UX and UI considerations. In most situations, the way in which the search controls what shows up on the left is not an algorithmic decision but one of UX/UI. Figure 9.2 provides an overview.

Consider how metadata is used in two ways at different times in the UX:

1. As metadata is applied to content, it allows users to choose from a controlled vocabulary of terms to apply metadata to documents when uploading; a strong controlled vocabulary will help prevent the dreaded "no results" page by linking synonyms and misspellings to the proper terms.
2. Allows users to narrow their search based on key concepts, built using a custom navigational taxonomy in your content system.

Figure 9.3 shows examples of how metadata searches in the DAM UI may be filtered.

Filter by:

❑ **Media Type**
   ❑ **Image**
   ❑ **Video**
   ❑ **Graphic**
❑ **Tags**
❑ **Brand**
❑ **Product Line**
❑ **Product**

Figure 9.3   Example of Search Filters in DAM

I believe that search should be taught to business application users once a year as a mechanism upon which to ensure that one is doing their best to share good search techniques with their users. The search tips in Table 9.1 are a great start.

Why is search so hard? Try to think of the content itself, and its arrangement with metadata.

In addition, the following search-based key performance indicators (KPIs) or metrics are invaluable when managing your entire content solution (see Figure 9.4).

Table 9.1 Search Tips

Keywords	Descriptors that can be tagged to an asset to aid in search and retrieval.
Using Quotes	Use double quotes to search full exact phrases in the quick search box (e.g., "products that shine")
Case Sensitivity	Searches are not case sensitive (e.g., "WidGET" and "widget" are equivalent searches).
Unique Identifiers	An efficient way to find an asset is by a unique identifier with such elements as a Packaging ID, Internal Product ID, or Trade Product ID. Depending on how your search is set up, you can then narrow the results with the metadata filters on the left side of the screen.
Wildcards	Searching partial words is not likely to produce any results (e.g., "widg" will not return results for widget). Wildcards help solve for this.
Asterisk (*)	Identifies multiple-letter matches in a search pattern.
Question mark (?)	Identifies single-letter matches in a search pattern.
Logical Operators	AND/OR/NOT

9.3 Metadata and KPIs

Business functions are siloed and only have visibility into their specific contribution to the overall product launch. Because each business function has competing priorities and little visibility into the overall process, they may not necessarily do their jobs in the most efficient order for each product launch. Furthermore, lack of accountability for the overall success of the product launch makes it more likely that the business function will work to optimize the KPIs of that business function rather than optimize the product KPIs. Finally, a siloed and vertical structure reduces the opportunity for cross-functional communication and collaboration, leaving the process more prone to errors.

More often than not, managers are responsible for launching products by submitting project requests and making sure the necessary updates are made to the system to be used by downstream business functions. There are individual workflow step owners and activity specialists who are responsible for setting up specific items in the systems. Nevertheless, the managers are only responsible for seeing the product setup to completion, which means they are not accountable for the end-to-end process or the overall success of the launch. This could be a great opportunity for some process reengineering to update your technology and improve UX to support the new efforts.

VALUE

USER ADOPTION

- Increase user satisfaction
- Create intuitive user interface to maximize adoption
- Increased brand consistency & compliance
- Increased speed of delivery, scalability and flexibility of digital capabilities

EFFICIENCY

- Measure an enterprise platform instead of multiple disparate systems
- Improve content rights management
- Understand cost of Non-Compliance
- Increase productivity to accomplish tasks
- Coordinate Upstream / Downstream product creation

COST SAVINGS

- Increase use and reuse of content
- Increase automation through implementation of technology
- Decrease content update costs through self-service enabled systems (web, email, social)

KEY METRICS

→
- ✓ % total active users across groups
- ✓ # of uploads / downloads / requests
- ✓ Asset ingestion metrics
- Standard web analytics (unique visits, pages views, etc.)
- ✓ Number and types of searches
- ✓ Login frequency

→
- ✓ Reduction in workflow times
- ✓ Reduction in support tickets
- ✓ Product launch timeline

→
- ✓ Labor cost savings
- ✓ Savings in agency spend
- ✓ Asset reuse percentages
- ✓ Total cost of ownership metrics
- ✓ Cost savings due to self-service improvements

Figure 9.4 KPI Example

In most situations I have observed, ideas are not thoroughly vetted before being introduced into the innovation pipeline because there is a large emphasis on speed. This reduces the likelihood that innovation is optimized in terms of potential risk/reward/return. Furthermore, because deadlines are tight and the process is rigid, there is no room to fail. Each step of the process must be done correctly and on time, but the product does not reach the customer until the end of the cycle.

Because innovation cycles are long, there is no room to get customer feedback or pivot until it is too late. You can implement a more agile innovation cycle in which information, or a minimal viable product (MVP), gets to the customer more frequently throughout the innovation cycle so that feedback can be incorporated, and the company can pivot during the cycle. This should improve planning accuracy and increase the chance of customer satisfaction and success. An MVP would be defined as the minimal version of the product (e.g., even conceptual brief/drawing) that can get the feedback necessary from the customer to proceed with next steps. The first example is a product idea—all product ideas can be refined only to the point that customers need to provide the amount of feedback necessary to move to the next steps or decide not to pursue. Similarly, this could be done with product specifications, artwork, etc.

I advise developing "personas" for your UX/UI plan.

Personas delineate the distinct user groups that will interact with the content system (see Figure 9.5). Considered through a UX lens, the configuration of who makes up what user groups should be defined not just by what they have permission to do or access *but also by what their actual, identified behaviors are in working with assets:*

- Do they perform actions in a linear fashion or jump between multiple tasks?
- What gestures do they take to complete a necessary task?
- How many steps are their actions composed of?
- What actions do they intuitively perform without thinking about them?

The key framework to keep in mind in defining a content system's user personas is to understand the character, workflow needs, and access boundaries in response to *actual identified behaviors*, as opposed to basing them only on desired or needed behaviors or on what users should or shouldn't have permission to access.

It is helpful to consider your content system's metadata, controlled vocabulary, and taxonomy components as data points that structure its information architecture. An information classification strategy that facilitates digital asset organization, storage, search, and retrieval is one of the most foundational components of any content system. Aspire to recognize metadata's value according

"Librarian" – Content Manager

"I want users of content management systems to be delighted with how effectively they can find and reuse assets."

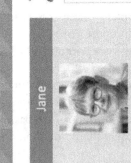

Jane

Content Manager

Manage assets and metadata

Enable intuitive asset search experience, while maintaining consistent folder and metadata structure

Responsibilities / Typical Activities

- Maintains all master and native content for the digital repository
- Ensures the content is entered and managed according to defined standards, which are applied consistently across the organization
- Work closely with brand teams, creative agencies and regulatory team members to ensure accurate and compliant content is used in promotional and packaging materials

Needs / Goals

- Assets are all current and have correct metadata
- Maintain a standard folder structure and metadata model for assets
- User-centric training guides for users

Key Scenario

- Bulk tag, audit and edit asset metadata
- Review and archive expiring assets
- Engage users on requested changes to metadata/taxonomy

Figure 9.5 UX Persona Example (Salt Flats LLC)

to a formal UX framework and understand that this fundamental concept in determining asset findability anchors natively within the context of UX.

The pursuit of easy asset discovery is deeply dependent on effective information architecture in the form of a smart metadata strategy. Be mindful of how easy it is for users to use a website or application; in particular for content systems, usability is the framework wherein features and functionality such as search, retrieval, asset distribution, and so on should be considered in relation to UX.

It is important that content system developers consider functionality development according to usability so that features complement and contribute to positive UX rather than sit divorced from it. User interface design (UID) encompasses the holistic design of interfaces and is composed of both the visual and interactive elements of how a website or application's pages and functionality look and feel. Be attentive to navigation and anticipate and complement how users will get around a system while minimizing redundant actions. Users will respond to a beautifully, intuitively designed system with limited functionality much more reliably than to a feature-packed application that is complicated to learn, difficult to use, or ugly to look at.

UID should subtly instruct users along a single, clear path when navigating the system. It is important that UID be developed so that visual and interaction design are deeply intertwined, and the two function as a seamless whole that facilitates ease of navigation and task execution.

UID should aim to eliminate any situation in which users experience frustration. Frustration causes users to abandon the system and even find a way to work around it—scenarios many content management practitioners can attest to witnessing. The goal is to reveal business priorities and continue to gain momentum in realizing these goals, run innovation sprints related to each identified long-term objective, and determine how to collect and track metrics that define success and keeps product teams accountable for end-to-end product launch success.

9.4 Conclusion

Metadata is the lifeblood of any digital asset ecosystem, and there is always time to put your metadata in order. The common business adage of "good data in means good data out" is true and cannot be overstated when considering search and UX. Having good metadata empowers search and creates positive user experience, which directly affects the users, which directly drives adoption. The notion of finding needles in haystacks is outdated; the key is good metadata—your data wants to be found by the people using your business applications. Without metadata you have nothing . . . metadata serves as an index to point your users, your people, to the content they need.

Chapter 10

Please Feed the Robots Good Data

*By far, the greatest danger of Artificial Intelligence is that
people conclude too early that they understand it.*[1]

— Eliezer Yudkowsky

10.1 Good Robot

There is a lot of interest and fuss over what the future holds for the management of information in modern business. The ideas of artificial intelligence (AI) and machine learning (ML) are no longer science fiction, let alone fiction, and have become applied practices and disciplines in business. And they both require and provide metadata in order to work. Machine learning is the ability of computer systems to "learn" with continually supplied data without an explicit programming telling the computer what to do. AI is the ability of a computer to display the apparent cognitive ability to think, learn, and problem solve in real time. This is both exciting and concerning: it forces us to realize that data is the foundation upon which these types of computer intelligence can be built. We want the machines—the robots—to learn and do more, but we must provide them with good, quality data in order for them to do that.

We need to get our metadata house in order to support this AI-based technology. Quality data = smart data = happy AI. Good robots.

---

[1] BrainyQuote. https://www.brainyquote.com/quotes/eliezer_yudkowsky_596818

In order to prepare for AI work, the determination of what metadata fields and relationships are most appropriate for AI integration using factors such as public domain data (e.g., color, shape, sentiment) and other business-centric data (e.g., product hierarchy, ingredients, etc.) is needed. In addition, the controlled vocabulary terms for AI usage needs to be reviewed for quality and authority to ensure that the accuracy and quality is there. Finally, we need to advise on the checks and balances, the ongoing maintenance, as performed by the "human factor" required in the testing and quality assurance of AI development. The robots should not work in splendid isolation, but rather with great human interaction the entire way through the process. This includes inclusivity, to strive for and do everything possible to remove race and gender bias in this important data foundation work. From technology, to transportation, to medicine, if data describes the world, then we must use it better to shape it, bring change, and provide visible race and gender equality. Without intention, data has no real power.

Search is everything, because it's all about access. Search is often misunderstood, if not downright underappreciated, when considering metadata and its influence on the effects of AI and ML from an end consumer point of view. In a Google-driven world, we all take it for granted that search not only works, but that it works to our satisfaction. That is to say, that we find what we're looking for within the first page of search results.

The "consumerization" of IT has led to a situation wherein there are often unmet expectations associated with search as business users familiar with the Google experience are challenged with a less than ideal search experience in their corporate IT systems. Search is not always the same experience, not only as the enterprise tool may not have an optimized search experience, but it is further complicated by data coming from multiple systems.

Since the early 20th century, people have collected, acquired, and maintained content, whether it be books, music, photographs, or other. This human practice has played a significant role in our identity in and relationship with our world. This has also become true for businesses—creating and collecting content in order to interact with other businesses and, more importantly, consumers. Companies now find themselves in a world where content is almost exclusively managed by digital systems and services. This is a busy, if not congested, place to be. Having end users at the center has been standard commercial practice for many decades, but delivering positive consumer experience is an ongoing dialogue that requires nurturing and practice.

Business needs data, and search is the way we navigate the data in order to procure content and, we hope, extract the meaning and value we seek. Data is just not data after all. We have *structured data*—that is, those identifiable pieces of data such as name, address, location, etc. that are found in database fields and structured for use. However, *unstructured data* is something quite different—it does not have the structure of a database or system. It may be an image, a video, a text file, a social media communication . . . all good content, but minus the structure that is needed in order for it to be easily found via traditional query methods.

The problem is that businesses are full of unstructured data. Content is produced without any metadata by which to search and categorize it, creating a library of files that cannot be properly utilized. An intelligent and robust metadata model and data dictionary will provide that reference for your work—a place to *"inquire within upon everything"*[2] for your business to search. That is all positive and good content to have, but it doesn't have the structure that is needed for it to be easily found via traditional query methods. The struggle in managing content within the digital world is as complex as the digital workflows underpinning the efforts. We can build trust through effective metadata and earn trust through good governance—the robots depend on it.

Data is a big deal, and is proliferating, and that growth is only going to continue exponentially. As it multiplies, organizations need refreshed, enterprise-level approaches to systematically create, distribute, and manage it. Hand in hand with this expansion comes increases in regulation on how organizations must manage and protect the privacy of their, and even their customers', information. Data is intimately associated with business transactions and, in turn, those associated actions by people, and it demands all our attention. Data is not just a technical challenge: the way humans interact with systems and processes must also be considered, and good security is designed with people in mind.

Managing data is a challenge for most organizations doing business in multiple markets. It is no longer sufficient to have a single policy for content storage, security, retention, and rights management. Each market may have its own set of requirements while also needing to collaborate with others. In addition, as new regions are addressed, new use cases may alter the traditional life cycle of digital content. From inception, there must be an understanding of data use possibilities so that metadata can be designed to support a broad range of use cases. While the ability to leverage content across markets improves its return on investment (ROI), the risk profile of content increases. To mitigate these risks, quality controls and rights management processes must be put in place.

---

[2] Anonymous. (1856). *Enquire Within Upon Everything: The Great Victorian Domestic Standby*. (R. K. Philp, Ed.) London, UK: Houlston and Sons. A Forbes article quoted Sir Tom Berners-Lee as saying: "When I first began tinkering with a software program that eventually gave rise to the idea of the World Wide Web, I named it Enquire, short for *Enquire Within upon Everything*, a musty old book of Victorian advice I noticed as a child in my parents' house outside London."

Conducting a systematic data assessment gives an organization insight into where it stands in managing its information effectively. It is the first step in creating a roadmap to consolidate content from various systems, apply consistent metadata, and maximize workflow, security, and ROI. All of this is done with a view to determining whether the organizational data and content environment supports organizational objectives and meets regulations. In this spirit of systematic, consistent data management, it is also important to define and manage the brand's purpose and function.

The data assessment should explore:

1. What is your data?
2. Where is your data?
3. What are you trying to do with your data?
4. How will you access (identify, retrieve, distribute) your data?
5. How are you able to use your data (rights management)?

As organizations grow in size, evolve, and take on additional global market opportunities, change will be the constant for the people, processes, and technology supporting business and marketing operations. Digital transformation plays a critical role in this change, serving as a focused center for content and operations management. Metadata, workflow, technology, and cultural context all affect operations and must be addressed for all organizations. Managing data is an opportunity to optimize your content's life cycle.

Data is all of our responsibility. The big deal with the *Cambridge Analytica*[3] situation is that the data was mistreated and not managed with the care it deserved. This is an example of where the misuse of data will happen and where trouble will occur. Data is hugely important, and it needs governance. If we understand that data is something that has value to the organization, then it is clear that controls should be placed on access to that data. If controls are not in place, or they are insufficient, then the consequences can be embarrassing and costly. The company could sustain damage to its reputation and could even suffer the loss of trust of clients or consumers.

Data provides a foundation for digital strategy. Creating the whole solution—and connecting it throughout your ecosystem—means that your digital assets can be part of this innovation by generating revenue, increasing efficiencies, and enhancing your ability to meet new and emerging market opportunities for your users. Embrace your content, understand all that you can about

---

[3] Wylie, C. (2019). *Mindf*ck: Cambridge Analytica and the Plot to Break America*. New York: Random House. 978-1984854636. This is a rather important book about the abuse of power and social media in our modern times.

what it can do, and never stop asking questions. All of this requires data integrity—ensuring that your information is complete, correct, and up to date. It is important that controls are placed on how, when, and by whom data can be created, modified, deleted, and used. We must treat it well and with responsibility.

Great content isn't really great until it is found, consumed, and shared. The opportunity for content owners, marketing technologists, and all those managing content lies in understanding the value of their content and how it can empower digital operations from creation, through discovery, to distribution. There can be no more reliance on or absolute comfort in what *was,* but only the willingness and ability to recognize that change is happening and to become an active participant in that change. For without such action, the risk of brand displacement, loss of intellectual property value, and the fiduciary irresponsibility of not knowing what assets you have will only make it worse to move forward.

Intimately knowing your organization's content and how to optimally manage it is at the crux of competitive advantage in today's world, where personalization and data privacy are essential. Responsible data management leads not only to the clear understanding of what you have but also to the ROI of managing that data effectively, enabling risk reduction, creating efficiencies, and increasing opportunities for content monetization. Now more than ever is the time for responsible data and good governance.

In order to have an effective process from which to work, you need to know your content and your business goals and objectives. Data, information, and content feed business—customer relationship management (CRM) data, finance, HR, customer data, and also rich media such as photos, videos, graphics, logos, and marketing collateral can all contribute to growth and innovation. Attention to how this content has been created, captured, and leveraged and how it creates an advantage is the key value proposition of a business's digital strategy. This foundation is the secret that can inspire and provide the groundwork for the transformative digital strategy that expands markets and manages complex, consumer-centered supply chains. The strategy is never finished but is a continual process of leveraging the collective intelligence of a network of consumers and providers for rapidly cycling invention. As long as change exists, a strategy will change. Success starts by defining what your customers and business aim to achieve and then creating a strategy that is flexible and well governed.

Technology is great when it is leveraged to transform data into information and then information into insight that can generate knowledge—something actionable and meaningful. Data provides the meaning upon which the processes and technology can be optimized. But if the data delivered does not match the user expectations, then the efficiencies of a personalized consumer experience are lost. What then about trust and authenticity? Technology is a tool capable of being used to achieve a specific goal. The tool's functionality has the capacity to produce satisfaction when used to perform a particular task. Understanding the needs of users and providing those touch points will increase the perception of personalization and improve the overall experience and allow machines to learn. The struggle in managing content within the digital world is as complex as the digital workflows underpinning the efforts. This provides the link allowing processes and technology to be optimized, and is hopefully where learning and intelligence may begin. The best way for AI to learn is by doing—working with good data.

In metadata we trust. The demand to deliver successful and sustainable business outcomes with our DAM systems often collides with transitioning business models within marketing operations, creative services, IT, or the enterprise as a whole. We see change everywhere—in people, processes, and technologies. Change is as present as it is pervasive. But have we become so busy with the proliferation of content and its associated processes that we have lost trust in our relationships? We need to recognize that change is coming, and we must see DAM as more than a tool for managing digital assets—we must embrace it as a critical component of the content and marketing technology ecosystem. More than ever, we need DAM to be not only the single source of truth for our content, but also the foundation upon which to build consumer engagement.

Trust in technology and the data flowing through its pipes will lead to greater participation, which in turn will increase the information's value and utility. Without trust and participation in your DAM relationship, no system can produce desired results. Trust and certainty that data is accurate and usable is critical. Leveraging meaningful metadata in contextualizing, categorizing, and accounting for data provides the best chance for its return on investment. The digital experience for users will be defined by their ability to identify, discover, and experience an organization's brand—just as the organization has intended.

Metadata makes data smarter, better, and optimized for use. The robots are waiting and ready to go, so let's give them what they need to do their job—a good quality data foundation in which to work. Data integrity is critical to AI and ML, as is trust and certainty that the data is accurate and usable. Be mindful of the people, processes, and technologies that may influence data and learning within business.

Content is critical to business operations and needs to be managed at all points of a digital life cycle. Leveraging meaningful metadata in contextualizing, categorizing, and accounting for data provides the best chance for its return on investment. The digital experience for users will be defined by their ability to identify, discover, and experience an organization's brand *just as the organization has intended.* Value is not found—it is made. Make your data meaningful and manage it well. Start with a foundation in data, embrace the transformation, and discover the value in content.

Chapter 11

Building a Metadata Strategy

The essence of strategy is choosing not what to do.[1]

— Michael Porter

11.1 Strategy Building Data by Data by Data

Metadata development is a strategic imperative in the endeavor to effectively manage and exploit a company's content and knowledge. The successful implementation of any content-related strategy—for data, digital assets, or text—requires implementation of a holistic metadata schema that is supported by technology, people, and process.[2] Metadata increases the return on investment (ROI) of a content system by unlocking its potential to ingest, discover, share, and distribute assets. Metadata is the foundation of a profitable digital strategy to deliver an optimized and fully engaging consumer experience. Content drives brand; regardless of what it is and where it comes from, content is what is driving your business. Metadata is the constant connection between your content and your users.[3]

---

[1] https://www.brainyquote.com/quotes/michael_porter_379016

[2] Horodyski, J. A formidable business case for metadata. https://www.optimityadvisors .com/index.php/insights/blog/formidable-business-case-metadata

[3] Garcia, T., Horodyski, J., Celso, J., Martin, J. (2019). White paper enabling content usage through rights metadata. https://www.rsgmedia.com/wp-content/uploads /2019/05/RSG-Media-Optimity-Rights-Management-White-Paper.pdf

Metadata is the foundation for your digital strategy. It is needed to deliver an optimized and fully engaging consumer experience. There are other critical steps to take as well, including building the right team, making the correct business case, and performing effective requirements gathering—but nothing can replace an effective metadata foundation for your digital strategy. As previously stated, you want your assets to be discovered, and they want to be found. Content may still be queen, but the user is also worthy because if you have great content and no one can find it, the value of the content is as good as its' not existing.[4] Metadata will help ensure that you are building the right system for the right users.

Now that the foundation has been set with definitions and key concepts, you can get to work on building an effective metadata strategy.[5] The path to good metadata design begins with the realization that your digital assets need to be identified, organized, and made available for discovery. To begin that design, the three key questions you need to answer are:

1. *What problems do you need to solve?*
   Ensure that you know the business goals of your organization and how metadata may contribute to those goals. Who is the metadata for? What business system(s) are being used and why? Where is it coming from and going to?
2. *Who is going to use the metadata, and for what?*
   Consider how much metadata you need, who it is for, and what the metadata is trying to do throughout the life cycle of the digital asset. If not done well, metadata may be expensive, so choose wisely. Less is not always more—quality and accuracy is the goal.
3. *What kinds of metadata are important for those purposes?*
   Make your model extensible—that is, allow extensions to the model's capabilities with relative ease. Knowing who your users are and what their workflow is will help guide the work for the short and long term, allowing for growth and optimization as your business needs evolve.

Metadata is neither magic nor an accident. It is purposeful and takes a strategic effort. These questions will undoubtedly lead to more questions as the

---

[4] Horodyski, J. (2018). Digital asset management: A foundation for digital transformation. https://www.optimityadvisors.com/insights/orangepaper-digital-asset-manage ment-a-foundation-for-digital-transformation?

[5] Horodyski, J. (2018). Digital asset management white paper. A guide to the lifeblood of DAM: Key concepts and best practices for using metadata in DAM. https://www .scribd.com/document/66594040/A-guide-to-the-lifeblood-of-DAM-Key-concepts -and-best-practices-for-using-metadata-in-DAM

justification and the business case for metadata develops for your organization. It is good to keep these questions in primary focus as the work begins and return to them for inspiration of and direction on what may be important to your organization's goals and objectives.

11.2 Timeline to Develop a Metadata Model

Caveat: *This timeline does not include pre-project planning. Time will vary greatly based on the complexity of the content and the organization.*

This timeline is based on over 20 years of metadata modeling work for organizations of a variety of sizes and complexity. The more organized the business is—having a "clean house" in which to work—positively influences the timeline. Conversely, those businesses with content chaos, information disorganization, shared servers of duplicitous, erroneous, and obsolete content will extend the timeline. In addition, the greater the content, the longer the work it takes to complete. I have been on metadata work assignments that have gone on as long as six to eight months to create a working metadata model because of the large amount of data to evaluate and process. Furthermore, the work may well take more time if there are multiple metadata models to review, and you may need a "crosswalk"[6] analysis to find the common terms, prioritization, and efficacy in usage.

Metadata is not a project—it starts, then evolves, and adapts with the business through all its changes. As long as there is more than one force at play, creating a standard will always be a challenge.

11.2.1 Building the Right Team

While there is no "I" in metadata, there most certainly is "team," for that is what is needed to do the work and to ensure success for the long term. This team may be the Metadata Working Group or other similarly named body of individuals working together to advance the program. This may also become the Metadata Governance Committee as the program matures. There are many good examples of members on that team, including the following:

---

6 A crosswalk analysis is a process used to identify and connect various similar or different elements, such as terms in a metadata model, to allow for a better understanding of the subject under review. It enables the connection of these elements for decision-making and planning to harmonize the terms in a framework for potential improved use and the enhancement of the access points to the subject.

- **Executive Sponsor.** Make sure that your champion understands the benefits of good metadata and is willing to support you both professionally and financially throughout your metadata program.
- **Business Analyst.** A business analyst will keep all work on track with larger business objectives and be able to balance the cost/benefit issues to decide appropriate levels of effort, as well as help to obtain needed resources, if those in committee can't accomplish a particular task(s).
- **Subject matter experts (SMEs) from each content group.** Every organization has those valuable individuals who have both the tacit and explicit knowledge of content throughout its life cycle. These are excellent people to get to know and learn from as you start your metadata journey. They have the subject matter knowledge of the business unit in which they work and understand the content from many points of view. They may well keep the committee on track with larger business objectives, as well as become metadata champions for the program from their business unit locations within the organization.
- **Metadata and/or taxonomy specialist.** If such a specialist exists in your organization (and you never know where they might be situated, especially in larger organizations), then seek them out and encourage them to participate in this program. It's a great thing to discover information scientists and librarians working in related subjects in your organization. They will bring their unique metadata skillset to the table and be an invaluable resource to the team.
- **You also need representatives from other areas:**
  - IT is an incredible ally and a welcome addition to the team to help you acquire the data from various content systems, ensure integrations are operating well, implement the metadata models to your systems, and more.
  - A representative from your legal team will help you identify and distinguish what you can, and in some situations cannot, do with the content you have and will help you determine the rights management and licensing metadata needed for your content.
  - The unique perspective of someone from a UX or UI background will help you and your team think about metadata not just as a binary construct, but as something to engage with, participate in, and create a positive experience with. One of the reasons there tends to be poor user adoption in content management systems is a poor UX/UI experience in navigation and search, so there is value in having UX/UI professionals as a part of the metadata program to create a meaningful experience for your users.

Once the team has been assembled, they may start considering working on the following items, both short and long term:

- Manage relationships between providers of authoritative source-controlled vocabularies in different business units and consumers of the metadata.
- Manage relationships with stakeholders and content groups.
- Create associated materials such as:
  - Metadata tagging/editorial style guide
  - Training materials
  - Corporate metadata standard
  - File naming conventions
  - Procedural and implementation governance documents
  - Testing for ongoing value of the metadata and taxonomy

11.2.2 Making the Business Case

Building a DAM or CMS or directing content management and marketing operations without a metadata plan is like trying to focus deeply with an undisciplined mind. Metadata increases the return on investment of a content system—and the content itself—by unlocking the potential to organize, discover, share, and monetize assets. Metadata is the key that unlocks the commercial potential of information, data, and intellectual or creative assets. Every piece of content has the potential to be exploited for a variety of purposes.

For example, an image tagged with descriptive metadata about gender, ethnicity, or age can be discovered and used for targeted marketing or for demographically specific content. A metadata schema that includes administrative information provides for targeted access control, allowing information and content systems to be used and searched by more users without expanding the risk of misuse. A well-designed metadata strategy also allows automated technical metadata, such as file type and size, to be leveraged to help creative and publishing teams speed the time to market.

Overall, metadata makes assets more valuable for a broad range of uses and users. In recent years, companies such as Amazon®, Netflix®, and Spotify® have built billion-dollar companies by investing the time and resources necessary to design and apply strong metadata strategies. For each of these organizations, metadata reflects a deep understanding of both their content and their customers. By committing these investments in metadata, these business giants have turned products, movies, and music into smart assets that can be searched for based on all manner of personal preference and monetized with amazing ease. This is the power of metadata: the cornerstone to the usability, scalability, and return on investment for any information or content management strategy.

The value and benefits of metadata are there for you to discover within your organization and shape your search story. Remember that building, testing, creating, and maintaining metadata are real costs. As an example, implementing metadata may require UX/UI changes or backend system change; ultimately, every metadata field costs money, time, and goodwill. There is no direct financial benefit unless the tagged content cuts costs or improves revenues. A good business case will aspire to:

- **Build engagement.** Identify the people, beyond management and project owners, whose support will be critical for implementation.
- **Manage expectations.** Determine what metrics can be produced about the strategy to increase the interest of stakeholders by aligning with their interests in order to show measurable progress and for reporting.
- **Create enthusiasm.** Create messages that empower management and the network build in the engagement phase to communicate the purpose of the strategy and how it is beneficial to stakeholders.

The benefits of your content cannot be realized without good metadata! Sell the vision of what the company will gain. At the core of any business case for metadata should include the argument for better, increased access to information—content should be easy to discover and not be a burden to find. Take the time to evaluate your business needs and your user requirements and develop a strong, valid business case.

11.2.3 Discovery and Requirements Gathering

In order to understand the metadata possibilities of the content under discovery, you need to understand the origins of the source: the creators and all those involved in content at inception, from creating, to reviewing, approving, and distributing content in your organization. It is important to conduct stakeholder interviews to determine not only the metadata project goals and metrics, but more importantly discovering what they know about metadata. Why is it used? How do they use it? When is it used? And, where it is used? This is the best, and arguably the most intimate, part of the discovery, as those who interact with metadata on a regular basis are able to share the details on such a close and special level.

You will also need to then turn metadata from those interviews into use-case scenarios and personas[7] to figure out what metadata would be needed and used

---

[7] A use case scenario is a representation of the action(s) involved to enable something, most often an event, to occur. Users may well need to take multiple paths at many times during these actions, leading to the final event, and may then determine more than one use case scenario is needed. A **persona** is a common term used in UX/UI design methodology as a fictional representation of someone—a customer, creator,

for later testing and analysis. You will need to insist that they *show* you what they do, and not just *tell* you. You may also need to conduct industry competitive analysis, if appropriate, to determine what others are doing in similar industries or product lines in managing their content. A detailed internet search will provide much good information on such things as product categorization, prioritization, and descriptions. Finally, these interviews will help determine the terms the business uses today to categorize information. As an example, consider the following metadata implications and applications they may want to manage:

- Search and retrieval
- Automatic reuse in new revenue-producing ways
- License tracking
- Digital rights tracking and management
- Automatic archiving
- Compliance
- Workflow management (versioning)
- What is the level of knowledge about metadata and taxonomy in the company as a whole? Where and how is data stored?
- What are the most important priorities for the metadata strategy in terms of business goals? (That may not become clear until you complete the interviews.)
- How many stakeholders and SMEs are there? How are they organized (e.g., one owner/SME per product line or more)?
- What types of politics or challenges exist between groups of owners and SMEs?

11.2.4 Content Audit

A content inventory is a process of systematically reviewing all the content you have and allows for a closer look at your optimization efforts to see how well you are meeting your business objectives.[8] It is both a tracking and assessment of what you have as much as it is an evaluation of its usage. In order to complete this work, discovery interviews with primary points of contact must occur

---

manager, etc.—involved in the work under observation. This persona will include the needs, goals, and behavior of the individual in order to better understand their individual actions, how they affect those of others involved in the process, and how improvements may be made.

[8] https://www.brightedge.com/glossary/what-content-audit

within each business unit to determine asset usage and workflow from inception, to creation, to review and approval, to use and reuse, to distribution and archives. In addition, it is important to evaluate other related content systems in MarTech, including collaborative sites such as SharePoint®, as well as internet and intranet sites. Finally, this asset inventory will provide a formal classification of each type of content and then define their characteristics, such as findability, usability, and ownership.

The content under review may exist in such elaborate locations as shared network storage drives, personal computers in a variety of named folders, currently used DAM or product information management (PIM), commonly used collaborative systems such as a SharePoint, old hard drives, and other unique places. It is expected that much of the content will be in a variety of states of completion, ranging from pre-visualization work, to drafts, to versions, and a variety of final forms, from final, to final_1, to final_2, etc. My observations over the years have taught me about "*final fear*"—due to an unfortunate combination of poor naming conventions and equally poor governance, multiple "finals" continue to be created. In addition, there will be duplicates and redundancies as a casualty of poor information management behaviors over the years stemming from a lack of good governance. As you begin to process all this information, be mindful of the following key metadata considerations:

- Does the terminology need to be created from scratch or rewritten?
- Is there a product information database of any sort in existence? And, if so, does it include their characteristics (name, description, number, etc.)?
- If there is a business website, how is it organized—products, solutions, roles, etc.? And look at both the internet and intranet sites for insight to categories, organization of terms, and prioritization in classification and navigation.
- How will users tag content? Do they have that software/interface in place today? Templates? Cheat sheets?
- What types of documents and vocabularies exist that provide insight into company focus and priorities?

It is good to know that there are software options to help this effort by analyzing the words, terms, and phrases discovered during this content audit process. And, depending upon the volume of content needing review, this may have to be created. That being written, a well-designed and managed spreadsheet will help this effort along and provide the ability to both quantify and qualify the content in ways that apply to your methodology and the goals and objectives of the metadata project.

11.2.5 Metadata Specifications

It is important to define the overall purpose of the content, based on the type of content being managed, its related workflows, who is using the content and for what purposes, with the goal of creating some possible content classification and management standards for your business. As shown in earlier chapters, the ability to define and understand metadata into the three categories of *descriptive, technical,* and *administrative* is the first step in organizing the content with metadata.

There are other things to consider when managing the metadata at the field level, as follows:

1. **How and what fields/elements will be used?**
   - As seen in Figure 11.1, some common fields include Title, Creator, Date of Creation, Date of Expiration, Location, Language, and Rights. For instance, the Title or the File Name is the most important piece of metadata because it represents the primary way that things are found.
   - Is the field required or optional? Single or repeated?
   - Are the field values text or alphanumeric?
   - How will proper names be listed? As an example, John Smith, Smith, John, J. Smith, etc.?
   - How will dates be recorded? I recommend year.month.day (e.g., 2021. 03.15).
   - Will the field be automatic or manual? Automatic metadata such as file size and file type occur at the time of asset ingestion. And, if manual, is it with free text, a drop-down menu, or radio button. And, is it using structured terms in the controlled vocabulary or predefined? (See Figure 11.2.)
   - Ensure you always have notes for each field to describe what the field is and for any other pertinent comments.
   - Will your DAM or other content system allow for versioning? Previous version? Modification dates? Comments?
   - It is important to understand if the content under review and its associated metadata are either a work in progress (WIP) or a final asset, meaning approved for use, published, and distributed.

Be mindful of the total number of fields to use when creating your metadata model. Metadata is about quality, not quantity. It is about accuracy, and that less will always be more. A good recommendation is to strive for your "top twenty" core metadata fields. There may well be good reason to have more,

Metadata Model example

Descriptive

#		Form of Entry	Status	Format	Field Length	Value / CV	System of Record	Definition
1	Description	Manual	Required	Text	250 chars	Manual	DAM	An account of the content of the item. This is to be in brief narrative form and describing the key areas of interest of the item.
2	Date - Creation	Manual	Required	Date	250 chars	Manual	DAM	Date of creation of the original resource.
3	Date - Release	Manual	Required	Date	250 chars	Manual	DAM	Date of asset publication for internal and/or external use in the live DAM system.
4	Date - Expiration	Manual	Optional	Date	250 chars	Manual	DAM	Date of expiration within the live DAM system.
5	Content Type	Drop Down	Required	Drop down	250 chars	from CV	DAM	Assets categorized in their business relevant context.
6	Audience	Drop Down	Required	Drop down	250 chars	from CV	DAM	Intended audience for use.
7	Channel (Media)	Drop Down	Required	Drop down	250 chars	from CV	DAM	Media used to deliver the information.
8	Language	Drop Down	Required	Drop down	250 chars	from CV	DAM	Primary language of the asset.
9	Keywords	Manual	Required	Text	250 chars	Manual	DAM	Keywords that describe the topic.
10	Creator	Manual	Required	Text	250 chars	Manual	DAM	Primary individual or entitiy responsible for the creation of the asset.
11	Location	Manual	Required	Text	250 chars	Manual	DAM	Primary location of the asset
12	Asset Title	Manual	Required	Alpha Numeric	250 chars	Manual	DAM	Primary and original name associated with the asset
13	Source / Business Unit	Manual	Required	Alpha Numeric	250 chars	Manual	DAM	Primary source of the asset within the business or organization

Technical

#		Form of Entry	Status	Format	Field Length	Value / CV	System of Record	Definition
14	File Format	Automatic	Required	Text	250 chars	Automatic	DAM	Format for the asset (jpg, gif, eps, psd, etc.)
15	File Dimension	Automatic	Required	Numeric	250 chars	Automatic	DAM	Physical dimensions of the asset (1072 x 890)
16	File Resolution	Automatic	Required	Numeric	250 chars	Automatic	DAM	Measurement for the sharpness and clarity of an image
17	File Size	Automatic	Required	Numeric	250 chars	Automatic	DAM	Size of the asset in the system (e.g. 260 MB)
18	File Length	Automatic	Required	Numeric	250 chars	Automatic	DAM	Length of the asset in the system (e.g. 45 seconds)
19	File Type	Manual	Required	Drop down	250 chars	from CV	DAM	Based on mime-type (regular, directory, special)
20	File Name	Automatic	Required	Text	250 chars	Automatic	DAM	File Name. Name given to the asset based on subject with user in mind.
21	Date Updated	Automatic	Required	Date	250 chars	Automatic	DAM	Last date the asset was modified
22	Date Added	Automatic	Required	Date	250 chars	Automatic	DAM	Date of adding asset to the live DAM system.

Administrative

#		Form of Entry	Status	Format	Field Length	Value / CV	System of Record	Definition
23	Rights	Manual	Required	Text	250 chars	Manual	DAM	Information about the rights held in and over the asset
24	Contact Information	Manual	Required	Text	250 chars	Manual	DAM	Primary contact name / role / team / agency for the asset
25	Agency Information	Manual	Required	Text	250 chars	Manual	DAM	Primary contact name / role / team / agency for the asset
26	Notes	Manual	Optional	Text	250 chars	Manual	DAM	An account of the content of the resource
27	Asset ID	Automatic	Required	Numeric	250 chars	Automatic	DAM	The system generated ID associated to an individual and specific asset

Figure 11.1 A Metadata Model Example

Controlled Vocabulary		
Content Type	Media Channel	Media File Type
Apps	Web	Images
Advertisements	Print	Videos
Animations	Mobile	Audio
Branding Guidelines	Social	Text
Brochures	Television	3D Models
E-Learning		
Games		
Interviews		
Logos		
Presentations		

Figure 11.2   An Example of Controlled Vocabulary Terms in a DAM

which is okay so long as they have value in better managing your content. There is an inherent financial consideration associated with metadata, as each field costs money to fill, validate, and maintain. (See Figure 11.3.)

Top Metadata Fields	
Descriptive	
1	Asset Title
2	Creator
3	Date - Creation
4	Description
5	Keywords
6	Channel
7	Location
8	Language
9	Source / Business Unit
Technical / Structural	
10	File Name
11	File Size
12	File Type
13	File Format
14	File Length
Administrative	
15	Asset ID
16	Rights Information / Copyright / Licensing

Figure 11.3   Top Metadata Model Fields

11.2.6 Workflow

The question to answer next is where the metadata comes from, and more importantly, who is going to apply the metadata to the content? A good action to follow is to document or map out the various digital assets that are constantly consistently being created and determine their various stages of creation from inception, to creation, to review and approvals, to final use and distribution. At each point in that process, metadata will be applied to the content, and it would be good to understand what the metadata is and who is doing it, whether they are adding new or adding to existing metadata. There may well be opportunities to streamline the metadata process along the way. Some helpful workflow-related issues include:

- Does all the input have to be manual, or are there some opportunities for automatic classification?
- How will you populate metadata elements with complete and consistent values? This is an argument for a well-maintained controlled vocabulary.
- How will metadata get mapped to the fields in the DAM?
  - Templates
  - Forms
  - Manually
- Is there metadata in headers, file systems, naming conventions, or query logs that could be extracted automatically to help populate the metadata fields?
- Who adds the metadata?
  - Creator at content creation?
  - Metadata librarian after the asset is complete, during the entire process, and/or as a gate keeper to ensure the metadata passes compliance based on the internal standards?
- Will there be checks and balances to ensure accuracy along the way?
- Automatic classification tools exist and are valuable for some types of assets. Results, however, are not as accurate as humans can provide, but they are more consistent.
  - Semi-automated is best.
  - Degree of human involvement is a cost/benefit tradeoff.

Metadata workflow is a key part of your strategy, as is directing the successful use of metadata during the life cycle of your content.

11.2.7 Quality Assurance and UA Testing

The final key element of an effective metadata strategy is *quality assurance,* otherwise known as QA, and testing of the metadata model you have created.

This includes both the application of metadata and tagging, both as content is being ingested into the DAM or other content system and at the other end of the process where content may be searched for, found, and downloaded. The QA and testing process is often overlooked, and yet it is critical to your success. Testing the metadata model should begin early in the process—if possible, start testing as soon as the first set of assets are loaded into the DAM and continue throughout the implementation.

The individuals you interviewed back in the discovery phase are excellent candidates to test the metadata, as they were the ones providing much of the information. Have them go through a few rounds of tagging assets and evaluate their effort on two levels:

1. The effectiveness of the metadata fields as well as the controlled vocabulary terms being used—do they work? do they need to be edited to increase their effectiveness?
2. The time it takes to complete one metadata record should not be a burden and should not take too much time; if it does, then it may well impact the ability of content to receive the metadata it so needs and deserves.

The time it takes to search for content using keywords and navigation through categories or facets should also not be cumbersome and prolonged. This is the opportunity to observe what happens with search, and then optimize with feedback.

- Elicit ongoing feedback using a Help or FAQ button or area of the DAM or content system.
- Use both qualitative and quantitative methods using online polls, surveys, questionnaires, and interviews.
- Look for items such as:
  - Consistency and appropriateness of metadata
  - Time to complete tasks
  - Reaction to search results
  - Usefulness of training materials

With regard to ongoing testing and evaluation of your metadata, there are key metrics (values) to measure (key performance indicators, or KPIs), as follows:

- Increased user satisfaction
- Intuitive user interface to maximize adoption
- Increased brand consistency and compliance
- Increased speed of delivery, scalability, and flexibility of digital capabilities
  - % metadata filled out

- ○ % required metadata filled out
- ○ Folder path analysis
- ○ Storage by business unit, etc.
- ○ Number and types of searches

As an ongoing mechanism to support your metadata value and manage risk, the following items are excellent indicators:

- User adoption, education, and support
- Metadata and taxonomy management quality
- Search performance
- Project management of changes to metadata/taxonomy, asset scope, workflow, system functionality, etc.
- Management of metadata governance council operations
- Facilitation and tracking of discussions and decisions
- Development of governance documentation
- Development of asset and metadata standards
- Interfacing and alignment with enterprise data initiatives
- Overseeing change control process

Finally, the use of good governance is essential to long-term quality assurance with your metadata and content. As discussed in an earlier chapter on governance, controlled vocabularies must change over time to continue being relevant for the products and/or services being offered by your business. What else must change when any specification changes?

- The master copy of the specification(s)?
- The assets that are already tagged?
- The UI that uses the metadata?
- The training material for users, catalogers, programmers, etc.?

There must be an agreed-upon change request form and a procedure for accepting or denying the change request.

11.3 Metadata Makes the Difference

Metadata is not just data about data but the spirit of an intellectual or creative asset. Metadata is the descriptive, administrative, and structural (technical) depiction of an asset. Metadata is a strategic imperative in the endeavor to effectively manage a company's knowledge. The successful implementation of any content-related strategy requires the implementation of a holistic metadata schema that is supported by technology, people, and process. It increases the ROI of a content system by unlocking the potential to ingest, discover, share, and distribute assets.

Metadata is not easy—it takes time, money, and resources to make it all work. Metadata is the key that unlocks the commercial potential of information, data, and intellectual or creative assets. And yet metadata is an asset unto itself—and an important one, at that. It provides the foundation and structure needed to make your assets more discoverable, accessible, and therefore more valuable. This is meaningful data to have.

We see change everywhere: in the people, the processes, and the technology within which we operate in business. Change is good, for it helps drive awareness to anticipate the effects of what is coming. Metadata is no stranger to this change. And while the future bodes well for managing content, there needs to be a recognition that change is perpetual, and metadata must be seen as a critical component of the corporate ecosystem, connecting systems and allowing for integrations to be successful.

Metadata must work within a transformational business strategy that involves the enterprise. Managing knowledge, rights, data, records, etc. brings different frameworks for managing content, and any content systems will be strengthened when working as part of the whole ecosystem. By understanding and defining fundamental goals and identifying information and content used by the organization, a good metadata foundation will help generate revenue, increase efficiencies, drive new uses for content, and meet new and emerging market opportunities. That's how you manage metadata for success.

Chapter 12

Metadata Maturity

Maturity: To do what's important and to ignore what's not.[1]

— Maxime Lagacé

12.1 The Metadata Maturity Model

A well-planned metadata schema establishes a foundational value, providing the conceptual architecture needed to make content more discoverable, accessible, and ultimately more valuable. Metadata turns video, audio, or graphic files into "smart" content that is available to reuse, repurpose, or simply inspire. After all, the full potential of an asset can only be recognized if it's discovered and exploited. The simplest search for an image on Google® would not be possible without it; it's the engine that enriches and drives asset discovery. When it is well done, it is imperceptible and intuitive.

A maturity model allows an organization to assess its methods and business processes against best practices and clear, agnostic benchmarks. The importance of reaching these benchmarks is a subjective decision based on business or other enterprise requirements. Once the appropriate level is identified, the path to achieving goals will be clear to all stakeholders. The application of a maturity model will not only establish an organization's placement on the maturation grid, but also, and more important, provide a precise, actionable roadmap for how to improve metadata strategy so the business may continue its growth and success.

---

[1] https://republicquote.com/quotes-on-maturity/

The Metadata Maturity Model highlights aspects of asset organization that can be used to increase information value in or between electronic systems. Comparing the level of an organization's commitment to each aspect is a useful first step in understanding the current state of metadata management. The self-assessment, according to its five well-defined levels, is a strategic starting point for diagnosing future goals and the tasks required to reach the future state. In addition, the Metadata Maturity Model provides visualization to help socialize content goals to management.

This model is a starting place and represents the benefit of collective years of experience in metadata analysis and digital content management. "A journey of a thousand miles begins with a single step," and the journey toward content management will bring benefits and opportunities for years to come. The Metadata Maturity Model will provide the benefit of creating a common language and shared ideology around the iterative process of refining metadata as a *continuous, evolving improvement and development* effort. Combining this with good governance and change management practices, an organization can evolve its metadata strategy to levels of great sophistication.

The Metadata Maturity Model proposes five dimensions of maturity across nine categories and five levels designed to provide a framework for understanding an organization's use and progress with its metadata and its content. The model suggests graded levels of capabilities, ranging from rudimentary information collection and basic control, through improved levels of management and integration, finally resulting in a mature state of continuous experimentation and improvement. The breakdown of this structure is as follows:

12.1.1 Maturity Levels

The five levels to measure maturity are:

1	Ad hoc	Exposure to the application of metadata, including managing content and content workflows
2	Organize	Casual understanding of content technologies, often starting in the form of content management systems and centralized, shared document repositories
3	Measure	Demonstrated experience with implementation of content management systems (e.g., DAM, web CMS, MAM) and core competencies, such as ingestion, cataloging, transformation transcoding, and distribution
4	Analyze	Managing repositories and workflow systems that are fundamental to business leadership with organized knowledge transfer
5	Optimize	Understanding and participating in forecasting enterprise needs in preparation of future business requirements

12.1.2 Metadata Aspects

There are nine aspects to consider as you evaluate your placement on the Metadata Maturity Model:

1	File and folder organization	The micro- (individual file) and macro- (folders) levels upon which your assets are organized.
2	User permissions and access controls	The level of secured access control(s) granted to users, as individuals and/or groups, to access identified assets. This includes role(s) definition and permission levels for access.
3	Descriptive keywords	The unique, defined, and recorded descriptive keywords associated with and attributed to the content being managed.
4	Search methods	The level of detail upon which the content is able to be identified and discovered by users from its infancy (managed by folder structures) to more mature settings (managed by data dictionaries and taxonomy). Search by name, classes, relations (search within a search), meanings, and user personas.
5	Workflow(s)	The placement and organization of the assets as defined within informal or formal workflow(s) within single or multiple business departments.
6	Standards, policies, and business rules	The rules and processes (e.g., formal policies) upon which the content is governed and managed from all users within the business.
7	Rights management	The unique, defined, and recorded rights management attributes associated with and attributed to the content being managed.
8	System integration	The physical and or digital location(s) of the assets and their level of integration with other systems within the organization (e.g., SharePoint®, BaseCamp).
9	Reporting and usage	The reporting associated with assets in their location and organization within the given structure(s) within the business.

12.1.3 Metadata Dimensions—The Collections

The vertical columns in the Metadata Maturity Model represent the *collection levels*, or the levels of maturity within an organization where content is managed.

Basic collections	File-folder hierarchies and pre-assembled collections using the desktop manager on a local workstation or server; meaning comes from the folder and file structures; users infer meaning from project file folders and ad hoc file names.
Identified collections	Categorized and tagged groups of reusable files, generally finished digital goods or renditions of varying size or resolution; collections resemble "buckets" of potentially useful items with little ability to cull contents into more granular and relevant sets.
Curated collections	Meaningful collections organized for anticipated user groups to access; curation emphasizes quality-assured files and task-based use case scenarios; most—but not all—curated collections manage vetted and approved finished goods but not work-in-process file versions.
Faceted collections	Sizable groups of diverse sets of files, templates, reusable assets, and business records optimized for a large, geographically distributed and diverse group of users to access. More than just a collection, this level integrates schedules and releases calendars across many project teams, surfacing "coming soon" items.
Semantic collections	Audience-relevant presentations and user experiences utilizing customer personas and micro-formats to assemble and bind media and content components into personalized finished digital goods; semantic collections include assets residing in other DAMs, content managers, and social networking platforms.

12.2 Metadata Maturity Level Assessment

The Metadata Maturity Model is a framework to be used and applied to current-state practice(s) in an organization. The first step toward finding an organization's place within the model is to document and record internal stake-holders who depend upon metadata, analyzing across functions and departments. It is also recommended to involve IT as early in the process as possible. It is likely that metadata "champions" or "stewards" will emerge who can play an active role in identifying pain points and communication requirements. Asset power users may emerge from, for instance, marketing operations, creative services, brand management, product management, communications, licensing management, or sales.

Metadata Maturity Model

Metadata Aspects:	Basic Collections	Identified Collections	Curated Collections	Faceted Collections	Semantic Collections
		Represent categorized and tagged group of reusable files, generally finished digital goods or renditions of varying size or resolution; collections resemble "buckets" of potentially useful items with little ability to call contents into more granular and relevant sets	Represent meaningful collections organized for known user types to access; curation emphasizes quality-assured files and task-based use scenarios; most but not all curated collections manage vetted and approved finished goods, but not work in process	Represent often sizeable groups of diverse sets of files, templates, reusable assets, and business records, optimized for a large, geographically distributed and diverse group of users to access; more than just a collection, this level integrates schedules and release calendars across many project teams, surfacing "coming soon" items	Enable personalized presentation and user experiences using customer personas and microformats to assemble and hand media and content components into personalized finished digital goods; semantic collections include assets residing in other DAMs, content managers, and social networking platforms
Files and Folder Organization	File and/or folder name on a server, shared drive, DVD, etc. May contain suspect data (corrupted, missing fonts or placed art); "right-click" on file reveals basic file properties if any	Basic level of organization and intelligence behind classification of content for use and potential reuse by identified users	Embedded EXIF and XMP data and file standards to provide enhanced file description and a richer user experience	Dynamic presentation of role-based collections, correlating asset profiles and user-engagement criteria; transcends file and folder structures	Structural metadata for related media components enable access to assets in context of the finished media product.
User Permissions & Access Controls	Self-directed basis	Create basic file sharing rules including passwords and read/write/delete server access	Identify, create, manage, and enforce rights and roles, regularly communicate these to team and users	Initial setup of user personas and structured levels of access and control	Customization and personalized experiences at department, team, and personal levels
Descriptive Keywords	None	Simple functional description such as "brochure" for a brand or market	More detailed descriptions of contents, treatments and possible applications	Detailed descriptive keywords and synonym rings (thesauri) aiding search	Includes fully developed synonym rings (thesauri) as well as relationships between terms (ontologies) that drive semantic search. Deeply enriched through search analytics practices.
Search Methods	Scan volumes and file directory of shared disk or DVD (Search PC hard drive)	Simple keyword search, visual scan of thumbnails with basic collections	Basic taxonomy in place to serve folder organization and meaningful search	Rich, meaningful navigation in place in search pages as well as across the system. Search index includes various systems for improved user experience.	Includes meaningful navigation within search pages, incorporating thesauri and ontologies into search experience. Indexes content from across the enterprise.
Workflows and Projects	Project or brand folder structure in shared drive or CD (Microsoft Project plans)	Basic project stages with simple routing and notifications	Full project lifecycle with robust notifications	Resource scheduling integrated to multiple workflows	Policy-driven resource allocation and re-tasking across a supply network
Standards, Policies & Business Rules	Identify and record as needed	Rudimentary level of standards and practices designed for a basic, useful experience	Semi-enforced and structured policies for assets pre- and post-system management	Enforced standards and rules for departmental and personal use	Creation of new standards and policies serving personalized workflows and business needs
Digital Rights	No system in place for rights management	Simplistic levels of usage rights: "ready for use," "in process," and "classified"	Administrative Metadata fields indicating rights, usage and licensing	Rights metadata refers directly to detailed enterprise policies for rights and asset usage	Use of DRM tools to serve creative process
System Integration	None. Much offline in physical media	Minor linkages with internal systems needed for operations	Basic integration with operations systems for approvals and workflow	Intelligent integration for creative processes and business logic feeding and supporting system	Increased collaborative tools for self-serving and group work
Reporting & Usage	No reporting mechanisms	No reporting mechanisms	Basic reporting in place	Directed reports tracking the use of assets	Personalized reporting tools and analytics for power users

PROGRESSION SEQUENCE FROM MATURITY PHASE TO THE NEXT WITHIN a particular type of COLLECTION
1. Ad Hoc > 2. Organize > 3. Measure > 4. Analyze > 5. Optimize

Figure 12.1 Metadata Maturity Model

(A description of Figure 12.1 can be found on the following page.)

The next step is to develop and administer a set of questions for stakeholders to provide detailed feedback about the current and desired future state of their metadata. These questions should be focused on workflow, use, creation, distribution, and management as well as key staff roles and responsibilities. At the end of the exercise, the organization will be able to find their place on the maturity continuum, exposing strengths and weaknesses to develop a plan of action to address the current level of maturity and prepare for future advancement.

Making a strategic business case for metadata and its robust management can be supported by developing a metadata return on investment (ROI) analysis. This should incorporate both **tangible** and **intangible** elements of metadata management. Diverse needs stemming from different areas may require **strategic** analysis to identify the areas that will most quickly yield a financial return from metadata. In addition, evaluating opportunities to see competitive advantage can be used to determine areas for continual improvement. Finally, the ROI needs to consider the **workflow** to reveal hidden opportunities such as increased integration, influence, and innovation.

Many organizations move too fast and think of something as grand as an artificial intelligence (AI) or machine learning project without the data foundation and mature metadata with which to support it. To start such a project requires good, quality data to determine what metadata fields and relationships are most appropriate for any AI work. Metadata matters because it is the tactical application of data to digital assets and content management, enabling creation and discovery for its distribution and consumption. Metadata demands attention for effective business solutions. The Metadata Maturity Model provides a common framework through which organizations can understand the use and management of their content's metadata. Applying the Metadata Maturity Model (see Figure 12.1) to content management initiatives allows for strategic understanding of current use and priorities for discovery, accessibility, and preservation of content. Keeping metadata relevant, usable, clean, consistent, and governed will assure that it serves the business.

Chapter 13

Metadata Is a Love Note to the Future . . .

Metadata matters, and now you know.

My aspiration is for you is to embrace the power of metadata for your work for the future in how you manage your content in all that you do. From the way you manage your Spotify® songs, to the way in which you observe the packaged goods in your grocery isle, to how you discover and find content at work and use and reuse that content in your business affairs. Metadata is the connection for people, process, and technology to work better together. Metadata is not the obfuscated, uncoded green lines of *The Matrix,* invoking fear and despair. But what metadata provides, when managed well, is the illumination of identification and meaning our content deserves, inspiring hope and confidence to users. It is simultaneously a snapshot in time and a love note to the future, identification in the moment and meaning in perpetuity. What it is at any given moment is correct, and what it is in the future may well be something more, mature and wise in its ways.

Technology succeeds when it is leveraged to transform data into information and then information into insight that can generate action and meaning. Collective actions build mutual trust among community members, establishing knowledge-sharing opportunities, lowering transaction costs, resolving conflicts, and creating greater coherence. Trust sets expectations for positive future interactions and encourages participation with technology. Communicating the meaning and purpose of why a technology tool is being used will build trust with its audience and impact positive experiences. Trust in technology and the data flowing through its pipes will lead to greater participation that will increase information's value and utility.

Technology is a tool, and it is capable of being used to achieve a specific goal. The tool's functionality has the capacity to produce satisfaction when used to perform a particular task. Understanding the needs of users and showing transparency in the technology, the people and the process will improve the experience and start the path to building trust.

Metadata provides the link allowing processes and technology to be optimized. But if the data delivered does not match your users' expectations, trust may be lost. The complexity of available data is compounded by the increasing rate of production and the diversity of data formats. Be mindful of the current situation and the challenges faced. More important, be mindful of the people, processes, and technologies that may influence transformation. Information, IP, and content are critical to business operations; they need to be managed at all points of a digital life cycle. Trust and certainty that data is accurate and usable is critical. Leveraging meaningful metadata in contextualizing, categorizing, and accounting for data provides the best chance for its return on investment. The digital experience for users will be defined by their ability to identify, discover, and experience an organization's brand just as the organization has intended.

History teaches us that the study of *diplomatics*[1] in archival studies posits that a document is authentic when it is what it claims to be. The Society of American Archivists definition of diplomatics reads, "The study of the creation, form, and transmission of records, and their relationship to the facts represented in them and to their creator, in order to identify, evaluate, and communicate their nature and authenticity." Its greatest modern proponent, Luciana Duranti,[2] reminds us to be mindful that *"the persons, the concepts of function, competence, and responsibility"* must all be considered when managing digital assets and trust, from creation to distribution. And so too shall all of us working in content management be mindful of these as we study our digital workflows, as we design our metadata models, and as we govern our content for the present and for the future. As Eminem so eloquently attests, *"trust is hard to come by,"*[3] so let's make it easier for ourselves and stop the misinformation and disinformation with transparency and integrity in our content as powered by good metadata. Trust in metadata.

Integrity of information means it can be trusted as authentic and current. When assets are allowed to move freely, the chain of custody can be lost, undermining trust that the information is original. By establishing rules around

---

[1]   Dictionary of Archives Terminology. (n.d.). Society of American Archivists. https://dictionary.archivists.org/entry/diplomatics.html

[2]   https://en.wikipedia.org/wiki/Luciana_Duranti

[3]   https://www.brainyquote.com/quotes/eminem_446850

originality and custodianship—or document ownership—assets can be relied on as the single source of truth. If we define an asset as something that has value to the organization, then it is clear that controls should be placed on access to information assets. If controls are not in place, or they are insufficient, the consequences can be embarrassing and costly. Possible dangers might include having the company sustain damage to its reputation, or it could result in the loss of trust for clients or consumers. Metadata is a strategic imperative in the endeavor to effectively manage a company's knowledge. The successful implementation of any content-related strategy requires the implementation of a holistic metadata schema that is supported by technology, people, and process. Metadata increases the return on investment of a content management system by unlocking the potential to ingest, discover, share, and distribute assets. Metadata helps us find the facts needed for that truth.

The opportunity in front of us is clear: we can invest in this effort and be a positive power of change. The benefits of metadata are real, and they are ready for you. You can dedicate this investment—this effort—in our people, processes, and technology. You can work hard to make the complex simple. The demand to deliver successful and sustainable business outcomes with metadata often collides with transitioning business models within marketing operations, creative services, IT, or the enterprise as a whole. You need to take a hard look at your marketing and business operations and technology consumption with an eye toward optimizing processes, reducing time to market for marketing materials, and improving consumer engagement and personalization with better data realization and analysis. In order to respond quickly to these expectations, we need content management systems to work within an effective transformational business strategy that involves the enterprise. Whether you view digital transformation as technology, customer engagement, or marketing and sales, intelligent operations coordinate these efforts toward a unified goal. An effective tool such as DAM is strengthened when working as part of an enterprise digital transformation strategy, which considers content management from multiple perspectives, including knowledge, rights, and data. Using DAM effectively can deliver knowledge and measurable cost savings, deliver time to market gains, and deliver greater brand voice consistency—valuable and meaningful effects for your digital strategy foundation.

Data is complex; it is growing. Organizations will need to show how they are acting responsibly in safeguarding it in order to build trust and confidence. The best way to manage your data is with the power and rigorous application of metadata. It is the best way to protect and defend digital assets from content clutter and mismanagement. You need to invest the time, energy, and resources to identify, define, and organize assets for discovery. Access is everything. Classification is meaningful. And action is needed now for the volume of digital assets on our

desktops, storage drives, shared drives, collaborative spaces, and content repositories throughout the corporate structures created to manage content.

Think of people when you think of metadata. Technology is decidedly
human. In the face of rapid workforce change, learn how to unlock value from
your greatest asset—your people. Think about the digital experience for users
and ensure they can identify, discover, and experience your brand the way it
was intended. It is a necessary defense. Integrity of information means it can
be trusted as authentic and current. If we define an asset as something that has
value to the organization, then it is clear we should place controls on access.

Think of process when you think of metadata. You, above, know your assets
and what they can do for you. Defining a strong digital strategy demands that
you collaborate with those who best know the systems and other resources
needed to release your assets' potential. Digital assets are varied and needed for
many reasons in your transformative strategy. As long as change exists in your
business, your strategy will change. It is never really finished. It is important
to be prepared for this and to ensure that your solution is flexible and well
governed. Successful collaboration starts by defining what your customers and
business want to do with digital assets and then creating the plan to achieve
it. After that, communicating how your assets are used to drive business will
inspire others, from IT staff to all users present and future, who seek to innovate
them for future use; it's access in action.

If data is the language upon which our modern society will be built, then
metadata will be its grammar, the construction of its meaning, the building
for its content, and the ability to understand what data can be for us all. Your
metadata is not going to be perfect in the beginning. Don't be afraid of making
mistakes. Think effective, not perfect, and always ask better questions about
your content. The struggle is managing within a data-driven world in which
the data is as complex as the digital workflows it supports. This landscape may
include not only your internal one but the wider geography of your partners and
third-party entities that crawl for your data on a very public internet. Add to
data complexity the increasing rate at which it is produced and the diversity of
the formats being used. You know that your assets are critical to your business
operations, and you want them to be discovered at all points within a digital
life cycle, from creation to discovery and distribution. To accomplish this, you
need a discernible sense of trust and certainty that your data is accurate and
usable. Metadata matters and is your best chance for a return on investment on
the assets you have created and also a line of defense against lost opportunities.

It is critical to understand that metadata is a snapshot in time representing
the business processes and goals at a particular time. In an ever-changing business environment, metadata must be adaptable and must evolve over time to
stay relevant to the digital assets that it supports. If maintained and governed

well, metadata can be a very real contribution to your business goals. Metadata is the foundation for your digital strategy. You want your assets to be discovered; they want to be found. Content may still be queen, but the user is also worthy, because if you have great content and no one can find it, the value of the content is as good as its' not existing. The path to good metadata design begins with the realization that your digital assets need to be identified, organized, and made available for discovery, and metadata will help ensure that you are building the right system, for the right users, at the right time. Metadata done well will ensure that you and your content will never be lost again.

Metadata matters.

Appendix

Metadata Manifesto

A public proclamation of my obvious intentions toward making metadata meaningful for all.

1. Metadata is a strategic action to effectively manage and exploit a company's knowledge.
2. Metadata tells you where your content came from, where it is going, and how it can be used.
3. Metadata needs to be understood and advocated by executive leadership.
4. Metadata unlocks the return on investment (ROI) potential to ingest, discover, share, and distribute assets.
5. Artificial intelligence (AI) and machine learning (ML) provide metadata and require metadata to work.
6. Metadata is needed for big data to be "big."
7. Metadata drives social media—the # (hashtag) is metadata.
8. Metadata reduces storage costs by controlling data redundancy and duplication.
9. Metadata provides rights management enforcement resulting in stronger revenue retention.
10. Metadata is required for any content-related strategy that is supported by technology, people, and process.
11. Metadata is already at work in your naming conventions, in folder structures, and in file names.
12. Metadata creates targeted access to systems and allows more workflows to be simplified.

13. Metadata allows you to accurately automate the distribution of your assets.
14. Metadata provides security and decreases the risk of misused assets.
15. Metadata provides rights management enforcement, resulting in stronger revenue retention.
16. Metadata moves business rules out of peoples' heads and puts it directly onto the asset.
17. Organizations that make decisions without metadata do so at their own risk.
18. Metadata is a human endeavor.
19. Metadata is the foundation of your content.
20. Metadata is the constant connection between your content and your users.

Glossary

AI	Artificial intelligence
CIA	Central Intelligence Agency
CMS	Content management system
CPG	Consumer packaged goods
CRM	Customer relationship management
CX	Customer experience
DAM	Digital asset management
ECM	Enterprise content management
ERP	Enterprise resource planning
EXIF	Exchangeable image file format
FAQ	Frequently asked questions
GMP	Good manufacturing practices
IP	Internet protocol
ISO®	International Organization for Standardization
IT	Information technology
KM	Knowledge management
KPI	Key performance indicators
MAM	Media asset management
MDM	Master data management
MIME	Multipurpose internet mail extension
ML	Machine learning
MMM	Metadata Maturity Model
MOOC	Massive open online courses
MVP	Minimal viable product
NCSA	National Center for Supercomputing Applications
NSA	National Security Agency
PIM	Product information management

QA	Quality assurance
RM	Records management
ROI	Return on investment
SME	Subject matter expert
SOP	Standard operation procedures
SQL	Structured query language
UGC	User-generated content
UGM	User-generated metadata
UI	User interface
UID	User interface design
UX	User experience
WCM	Web content management
WIP	Work in progress
XMP®	Extensible metadata platform

Index